KT-464-371

NETBALL

Steps to Success

Wilma Shakespear
Director, Queensland Academy of Sport

Human Kinetics

Withdrawn
TO49907

796.32

Library of Congress Cataloging-in-Publication Data

Shakespear, Wilma, 1943-
    Netball : steps to success / Wilma Shakespear.
        p.   cm. -- (Steps to success activity series)
    ISBN 0-87322-984-3
    1. Netball.   I. Title.   II. Series.
GV889.6.S53   1997
796.324--dc21   97-7790
                                                                     CIP

ISBN: 0-87322-984-3

Copyright © 1997 by Human Kinetics Publishers, Inc.

All rights reserved. Except for use in a review, the reproduction or utilization of this work in any form or by any electronic, mechanical, or other means, now known or hereafter invented, including xerography, photocopying, and recording, and in any information storage and retrieval system, is forbidden without the written permission of the publisher.

Developmental Editor: Kirby Mittelmeier; **Assistant Editor:** Jennifer Stallard; **Editorial Assistants:** Amy Carnes and Jennifer Hemphill; **Copyeditor:** Sonja Draeger; **Proofreader:** Karen Bojda; **Graphic Designer:** Keith Blomberg; **Graphic Artist:** Kathy Boudreau-Fuoss; **Cover Designer:** Jack Davis; **Photographer (cover):** Wilmer Zehr—equipment provided by Mitre Sports International, LTD; **Illustrator:** Keith Blomberg; **Mac Artist:** Tim Stiles; **Printer:** Versa Press

Instructional Designer for the Steps to Success Activity Series: Joan N. Vickers, EdD, University of Calgary, Calgary, Alberta, Canada

Human Kinetics books are available at special discounts for bulk purchase. Special editions or book excerpts can also be created to specification. For details, contact the Special Sales Manager at Human Kinetics.

Printed in the United States of America   10   9

Human Kinetics
Web site: www.HumanKinetics.com

United States: Human Kinetics, P.O. Box 5076, Champaign, IL 61825-5076
800-747-4457
e-mail: humank@hkusa.com

Canada: Human Kinetics, 475 Devonshire Road, Unit 100, Windsor, ON N8Y 2L5
800-465-7301 (in Canada only)
e-mail: orders@hkcanada.com

Europe: Human Kinetics, 107 Bradford Road, Stanningley
Leeds LS28 6AT, United Kingdom
+44 (0) 113 255 5665
e-mail: hk@hkeurope.com

Australia: Human Kinetics, 57A Price Avenue, Lower Mitcham, South Australia 5062
08 8277 1555
e-mail: liaw@hkaustralia.com

New Zealand: Human Kinetics, Division of Sports Distributors NZ Ltd.
P.O. Box 300 226 Albany, North Shore City, Auckland
0064 9 448 1207
e-mail: blairc@hknewz.com

Contents

PREFACE

There is something magical about a netball centre in Australia: 20 to 30 courts abuzz with players trying to outmanoeuvre and outwit their opponents; the constant sound of umpires' whistles; the concentration on the faces of the shooters and the desperation of the defenders. It's all about having fun and all part of the regular scene at the local courts. While the number of local courts may vary considerably throughout the netball world, the fun and competitiveness remain constant.

Netball is first and foremost a game of participation. Netballers love to play, to compete and to pit their talents and strategies against their opponents. They also love devising game plans. Hours are spent developing tactics, and probably even more hours are whiled away on the post-mortem of a match.

Netballers have a highly developed sense of teamwork. They understand that to be successful they need to combine their individual talents with those around them—they need to make allowances for the strengths and weaknesses of others so that the skills of all are greater and more effective than the skills of one.

Developed from humble beginnings as a game for schoolgirls, netball in the '90s is endeavouring to find its place as a national and international sport. Its greatest asset in this quest is the athleticism of its leading athletes, all of whom can match skills with sports' top heroes worldwide: Sandra Edge, the agile New Zealand centre; Vicki Wilson, Australia's goal-shooting legend; and Irene Van Dyk, the sensational South African shooter. One finds a wealth of highly developed talent in the national teams, the top of the netball scale, all intent on becoming the world's best.

In recent years, the advent of televised games has generated much interest in the sport within Australia. New Zealand has long enjoyed good ratings from live telecasts of major matches. In other countries, major domestic and international matches are reaching an ever-increasing audience. It is a very exciting time for netball! Many opportunities are emerging that will enable this game—a game that has a place for everyone—to receive the acknowledgments it so richly deserves.

For my part, I will always remain grateful for the opportunities this sport has given me. At 19 years of age I was selected in my first Australian national team. Travelling to England to compete had a huge impact on my life. In an era when most females set their sights on marriage, a home and family, my first World Tournament showed me there was also another larger world that I could be part of.

As an international athlete and coach, the game gave me so many valuable life experiences. The joy of victory and the disappointment of defeat are two that instantly spring to mind. Learning to maintain dignity when we lost and humility when we won helped make me a better, stronger person. Making a career change to sports administration was a relatively simple task because netball had given me such a rich background of experiences to draw from.

When I look back on my career, some of my fondest memories come from my early playing days. These memories include the patience that my father had with his netball-mad family, and the pride we all took from the unique appointment of Mum and myself as manager and coach (respectively) of Australia's National Team at the World Tournament held in Jamaica in 1971. Winning that one was something special.

The other great highlight in my career was the opportunity to establish the netball program at the Australian Institute of Sport. They were heady days. The impact on netball, particularly within Australia, was significant and could not have been achieved without the talent of our staff, Gaye Teede, Margaret Caldow and Sue Hawkins, and the support of my own family, Peter, David and Susan.

In writing this book I have been assisted by Margaret Caldow. Her expertise in goal shooting is acknowledged internationally and greatly appreciated by her old friend, particularly when writing step 4.

THE STEPS TO SUCCESS STAIRCASE

Netball is a team game, which means there are two aspects of becoming a successful player. First you have to learn the skills of the game—how to catch and throw, to shoot for goals, and to move in attack and defence. Then comes the real challenge: to use these skills effectively with other team members to produce a winning netball team.

The steps presented in this book are to guide you along your way to learning and perfecting your netball skills. The first few steps provide a foundation—a solid base of performance and movement skills you need to attack and defend effectively. Constantly polish these basic skills, for if you can hone them to perfection they will not let you down. As you progress you will be able to combine these skills and then test them out under match-like conditions. The next steps make sure that before you prepare to play competitively, you understand the basic rules of the game and team strategy. The final steps look specifically at each third of the court. They will enable you to enhance your work in your specialist area once you begin playing competitively.

Drills provided in each step are graduated from simple to complex. You should aim to work at maximum intensity on each drill. Once you have reached your Success Goal, move on. Challenge yourself by tackling a new drill or a more complex version of the one you have just done. Don't forget to add your own drills too—the game calls for you to be creative, so introduce your own flair to the training schedule.

Don't be surprised if you make some mistakes along the way. When you start putting new skills into practice they don't always fall into place. You will need to work hard, so put your best effort into training. When a routine breaks down, return to the basic skill, work it until you are confident, then tackle a more demanding task. Never walk away from a difficult passage—learn to work your way through it.

Once you feel that you are really doing well with the basic skills, you will find it becomes more productive to train with a partner or a small group. When you begin team play, most of your training will be done with your team members.

As you climb the steps to netball success, follow the same sequence for each step:

1. Read the explanations of what the step covers, why the step is important, and how to execute the step's focus, which might be a basic skill, concept, tactic, or combination of all three.
2. Follow the numbered illustrations showing exactly how to position your body to execute each basic skill successfully. There are three general parts to each skill description: preparation (getting into the right position), execution (performing the skill that is the focus of the step), and follow-through (finishing position).
3. Look over the common errors that might occur and recommendations for how to correct them.

4. Read the directions, the "Success Goals" and the "Success Check" items for each drill. Practice accordingly and record your scores and improvement. You need to meet the Success Goal for each drill before moving on to practice the next one because the drills are arranged in an easy-to-difficult progression. This sequence of drills is designed specifically to help you achieve continued success. Pace yourself by adjusting the drills to either increase or decrease their difficulty, depending on your skill level.

5. As soon as you can reach all the Success Goals for one step, you're ready for a qualified observer, such as your teacher, coach, or trained partner, to evaluate your basic skill technique against the "Keys to Success" found at the beginning of each step. This provides a qualitative, subjective evaluation of your basic technique. By focusing on correct technique, you can enhance your performance. Ask your observer to suggest improvements.

6. Repeat this procedure for each of the 11 Steps to Success, then rate yourself according to the directions for "Rating Your Progress".

Now, to begin! Read the next chapter to find out what the game of netball is all about, then take the steps toward becoming a skilled performer and a valued member of a team playing this great game.

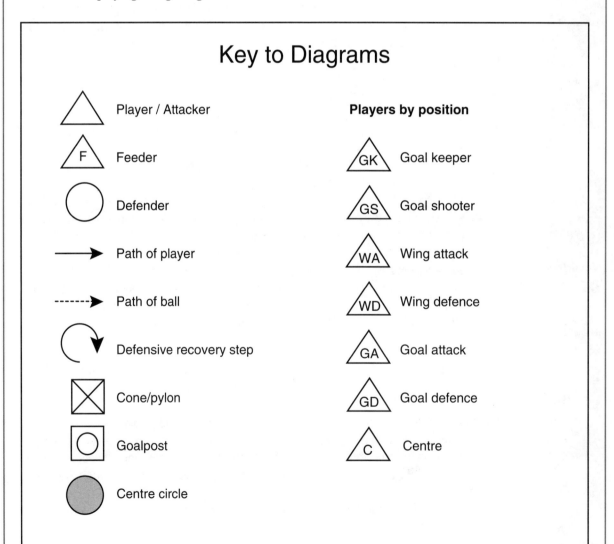

Key to Diagrams

△	Player / Attacker	**Players by position**	
△F	Feeder	△GK	Goal keeper
◯	Defender	△GS	Goal shooter
→→	Path of player	△WA	Wing attack
------▸	Path of ball	△WD	Wing defence
↻▼	Defensive recovery step	△GA	Goal attack
⊠	Cone/pylon	△GD	Goal defence
▣	Goalpost	△C	Centre
⬤	Centre circle		

THE GAME OF NETBALL

I remember a group of us explaining the game to some interested Americans as we sped towards the West Indies on a tour with the team from the Australian Institute of Sport. "Ah, netball", they said, reading our uniform pockets, "Now is that the game where you hit the ball over the net?"

"No", we replied, "that's volleyball".

"Well then", they asked, "what is it?"

We found the easiest way to describe this game of ours was to start with a game they knew well—basketball—and to explain the similarities and differences. Given that the history of netball traces back to the man credited with inventing basketball, Dr. James Naismith, it seemed a fairly logical way to go.

A netball court is a little longer than a basketball court and is divided into three areas of equal size. There are 7 players from each team on court, 14 in all. Unlike basketball, netball players have specific areas on the court in which they are permitted to move. Netballers must pass the ball, rather than dribble it, and are only allowed to take one step with the ball before releasing it. Only a team's two shooters may score goals—which they do by shooting the ball through a hoop—but they do it without using a backboard. When a goal is scored, the game is restarted with a pass from the centre of the court, so mid-court play assumes greater emphasis than in basketball.

Like basketball, netball is fastmoving and highscoring; however, unlike basketball, it is strictly non-contact.

The Americans were curious, as are most people when they first learn about netball. They had difficulty imagining how you could score accurately without using a backboard. They also wondered how the game could be so speedy if players could not run with the ball and were confined to certain areas of the court. "It's our reflexes", the players explained, "they're razor sharp. We move like greased lightning". The players smiled. The Americans studied the athletes for a while, then smiled back. They believed the players meant what they said.

A Short History of Netball

When Dr. Naismith invented basketball in an American YMCA in 1891, it is unlikely that he realised that he had also given birth to netball—today the most popular women's sport in Australia and New Zealand, and gaining an ever-increasing following in the United Kingdom, the Caribbean, Asia and Africa.

When the students of Madame Osterberg's College of Physical Training at Hampstead, England, were first introduced to netball in 1895—then known as women's basketball—there were no printed rules and no court lines, circles, or boundaries. The goals were two wastepaper baskets hung on walls at each end of the hall. Because the baskets were closed at one end, the umpire had to climb a ladder to retrieve the ball each time a goal was scored. Spectators found this highly amusing. Players surely felt it wasted time.

Two years later the game was first played outdoors. The English students introduced rings instead of baskets, a larger ball, and divided the ground into three equal playing areas known as thirds of the court. The women who played wore long, flowing skirts and leg-of-mutton sleeves. The first recorded rules were published in England in 1901.

From such humble beginnings the game was introduced to other countries by schoolteachers and members of the religious teaching orders, who, at the time, travelled to all the far-flung corners of the British Empire. Netball arrived in Australia and New Zealand at about the turn of the century.

The first national association was that of New Zealand in 1924, followed by England's in 1926 and Australia's in 1927. Although geographically close, New Zealand and Australia continued to alter rules without reference to each other until 1938, as did other netball-playing countries of the Commonwealth for years after that. Of course, this made international competition difficult.

In 1960 an international code of play was introduced, and within a few years the game was called netball worldwide. The first World Tournaments were held at Eastbourne in England in 1963, where Australia and New Zealand established themselves as the sport's leading nations. In a thrilling encounter, Australia defeated its Kiwi rivals by a single goal to claim the first world crown. Since that time, Australia has captured all but three of the nine world titles held to date. New Zealand has taken the title twice. In the 1979 series, there was a three way tie between New Zealand, Australia, and Trinidad and Tobago.

Like the Olympics, the Netball World Championships are staged every four years. In the intervening time, major international competitions are arranged between leading nations, and regional championships are also regular fixtures.

Today the game is governed by the International Federation of Netball Associations (IFNA). There are currently some 40 member nations of the IFNA, most of whom are members of the British Commonwealth of Nations. Each national organisation drives the sport within its own country.

Within Australia, state, regional and country associations cater to the sport's one million players. The emergence of leagues run by private Indoor Sports Centre operators indicates that the sport has a growing business appeal. The top international and national events now receive television coverage, and the advent of pay TV should increase netball's exposure even further.

One of the major challenges for the game today is to develop its appeal internationally, and some interesting programs are emerging. Australia recently undertook promotional tours in China and Japan. England is targeting European countries, while New Zealand has a long tradition of assisting the nations of the South Pacific. Netball needs to establish a sound development in countries such as these and become a mainstream sport in North America and Africa. The re-entry of South Africa is an encouraging sign that IFNA is working towards expanding the game's international player base.

Dr. Naismith would no doubt be amazed to learn that the game he invented was taken to England, where it was refined for women and given a new name: netball. Today this popular game is played not only by women—men are taking to the courts as never before to participate in league play. Besides men's leagues, mixed netball is one of the game's fastest growth areas in Australia's Indoor Sports Centres. If this experience is repeated around the netball world, then a whole new generation of players will be introduced to the game.

The future holds much promise for netball as it moves away from its schoolgirl image and gains acceptance in the fast lane of corporate and international sport.

Playing the Game

A netball team consists of seven players, each having a specific position that restricts them to movement within specific areas—or thirds—of the court. Letters worn by the players on their tops identify their positions. This helps the two umpires who control the game to see when players travel outside their areas.

The object of the game is to score more goals than the opposition. Goals are scored by projecting the ball above then completely through a ring attached to a goalpost. Goals can be scored only by one of the team's two "shooters" standing within the team's goal circle. The goalposts are 3.05 metres (10 feet) high, and the ring has a net attached to it, which makes it easy to see when a goal is scored. Each goal scores one point.

The court measures 30.5 metres (100 feet) long and 15.25 metres (50 feet) wide (diagram 1). It is divided by lines, called "transverse lines", into even thirds: two goal thirds and a centre third. The centre third contains a centre circle 0.9 metres (3 feet) in diameter. At either end of the court (in each goal third) is a goal circle 4.9 metres (16 feet) in radius, and a goalpost centred on the goal line. All lines on the court measure 50 millimetres (2 inches) wide and are part of the playing area.

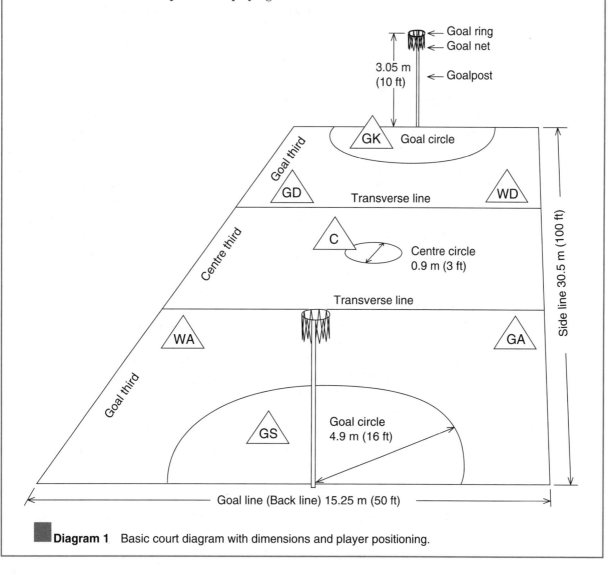

Diagram 1 Basic court diagram with dimensions and player positioning.

For the purpose of umpiring, the length of the court is divided in half across the centre from sideline to sideline. Each umpire is responsible for controlling and giving directions in one half of the court, from the centre to the goal line and the whole of the sideline. Both work together to ensure the game flows smoothly and that players receive clear, concise decisions. At the start of the game the umpires toss to decide which goal end each shall control.

Play begins, after the umpire's whistle, with a centre pass (from the centre circle). Before the whistle, all players must be in their starting thirds. That means the only players in the centre third are the two centres. All other players stand behind the transverse lines at either end of the court (diagram 1). After the whistle sounds, the players enter the centre third to contest the first pass.

Netball is, by design, a passing game; dribbling and running with the ball are not allowed. Through quick and accurate passing, the attacking team moves the ball down the court towards their goal. The ball must be handled in each third of the court as it travels from end to end. Because a player is only allowed one step with the ball and must release it within three seconds, proper positioning to receive and deliver passes quickly and cleanly is all important for the attacking team. The aim of the team in defence is to anticipate and position itself to intercept a pass or to limit the attacking team's shooting opportunities. Netball demands that all team members have sound attacking and defending skills and are able to switch quickly from one role to the other as team possession changes.

Netball is a non-contact sport, and the rules and penalties for defending reflect this. When a player has possession of the ball, the opponent must clear a distance of 0.9 metres (3 feet)—stepping back with a move called a recovery step—before attempting to defend. Defending within this defined distance is called *obstruction* and results in a penalty pass or shot being awarded against the infringer. Contact—hitting, pushing or bumping—that interferes with play brings the same penalty.

After the ball reaches a shooter within the team's goal circle, a shot at goal can be taken. Netball shooters use a stationary shooting technique. This sudden stopping to shoot for goal provides an immediate change of tempo from the speed of down-court play. When the ball leaves the shooter's hands, the action starts again. Defenders try to intercept the shot or position themselves for a rebound. If the attempt to shoot a goal is unsuccessful and the ball rebounds into court, then play continues; if the ball goes out of court, then a throw-in is taken. One goal is scored from each successful shot. A centre pass restarts play after each goal with possession of the centre pass alternating from one team to another throughout the match.

A scorer records both teams' goals and a timekeeper has responsibility for the duration of play. There are four quarters of even time for an official match. The international timing is four quarters of 15 minutes. (When a team plays two matches on the same day, the matches are reduced to two 20-minute halves.) There are many local time variations used throughout the netball world. Juniors begin with four five-minute periods of play. Ten-minute quarters are also popular, particularly in school competitions. 15- or 20-minute halves are also common.

The rules of netball have been simplified for younger players in recent years. Modified rules are definitely the best way for young players to learn. As skills, tactics and drills are described throughout the book, the applicable rules are discussed. For a more detailed description of netball rules of play, see Appendix.

Like many team sports, netball has some rules that require quick interpretation and judgment by umpires during the game. Of course, this is the area that creates controversy and excitement and allows the fans a chance to air their feelings. The players, on the other hand, rarely react to dubious calls. Given that the time players can handle a ball is restricted to three seconds, their focus moves quickly to the next pass. Besides, a player who brings the game into disrepute can be sent off the court.

Netball is played on a variety of surfaces. Sprung wooden flooring is ideal, but often the cost is prohibitive. Grass, asphalt, and commercially developed surfaces that add a rubberised component to asphalt such as flexi-pave are currently among the most common playing surfaces.

The Players

While each player must be adept at the skills involved in both attacking and defensive play, the seven positions and their respective playing areas (see accompanying diagrams) determine each player's specific roles and contribution to the team.

Goal Shooter (GS): The mainstay of the team's shooting, the goal shooter position requires an accurate shot and the ability to create space for the pass to be taken safely. It's important for the goal shooter to develop a variety of attacking options and, after shooting, to chase the ball to the post and rebound consistently.

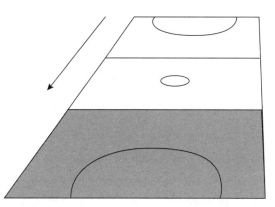

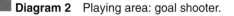 **Diagram 2** Playing area: goal shooter.

Goal Attack (GA): The secondary shooting role, the goal attack needs a solid shooting technique, an ability to provide attacking opportunities in the shooting third and an ability to assist in the centre-court attack when needed. The goal attack must be a versatile athlete who can defend strongly in two thirds of the court.

Wing Attack (WA): The wing attack needs to have a good feel for positioning of the shooters and accurate passing skills. These are needed to "feed" the ball precisely to the team shooters. At the centre pass the wing attack is the key player. It's important for the wing attack to develop strong, explosive moves to beat opponents across the line and take the ball.

Centre (C): The racehorse of the team—one who can run all day—the centre must possess good, balanced attacking and defending skills, and a reliable pass. A good awareness of all players on court and the space in which they are working is important. By reading the opponents' down-court play, the centre must be able to recognise where the defensive gaps are and to move into them quickly while always looking for that loose ball to pounce on.

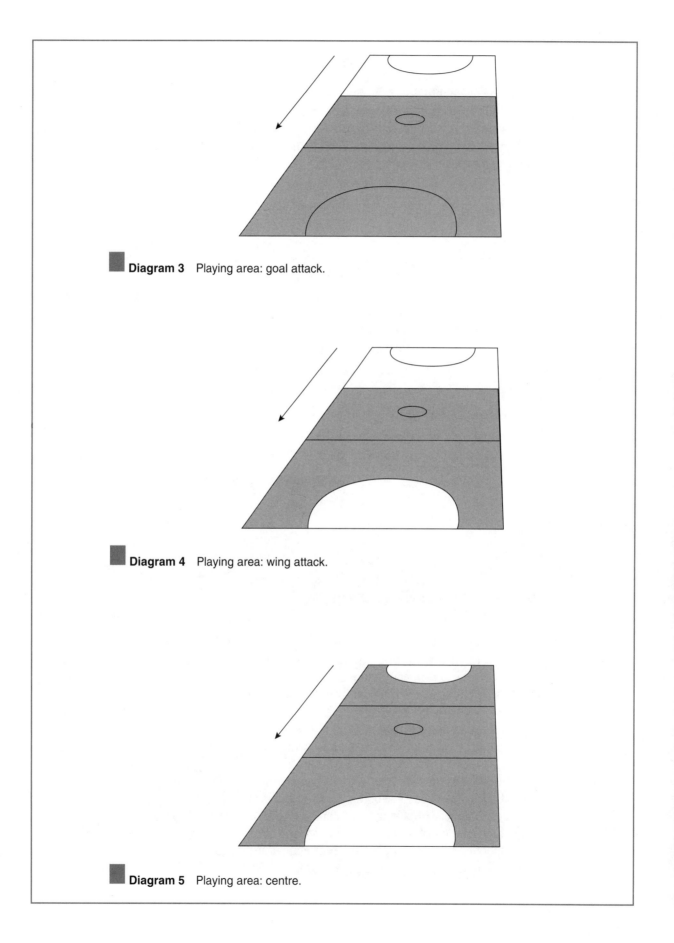

Diagram 3 Playing area: goal attack.

Diagram 4 Playing area: wing attack.

Diagram 5 Playing area: centre.

Wing Defence (WD): The wing defence is the first line of the players specialising in defence. The wing defence needs a thorough knowledge of defence strategy to defend the centre third and the top of the goal third and must possess the ability to stick with an opponent. The wing defence should try to out-think the wing attack because to outrun them is very difficult. The wing defence also has an important attacking role through mid-court.

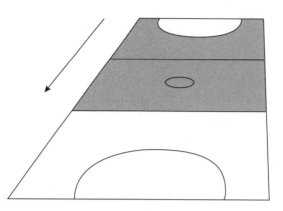

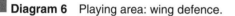 **Diagram 6**   Playing area: wing defence.

Goal Defence (GD): The mobile defence player who concentrates defensive pressure in the back third, the goal defence must react quickly to opponents' moves, knowing where the most likely intercepts are. The goal defence must think smart and concentrate on positioning to direct the attacker away from the play. Remember: you are trying to restrict your opponent's scoring opportunities.

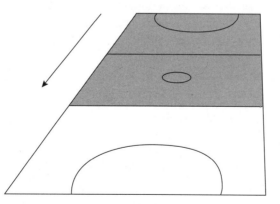

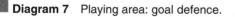 **Diagram 7**   Playing area: goal defence.

Goal Keeper (GK): The last line of defence, the goal keeper tries to counter the opposing shooter—particularly in the goal circle. Goal keepers must know where the goalpost is at all times and keep opponents as far from it as possible by positioning well. A good goal keeper defends every shot and jumps strongly for rebounds.

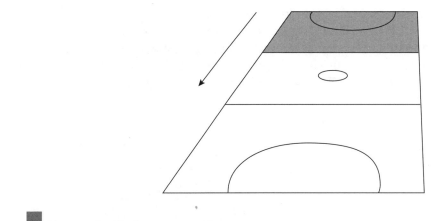

Diagram 8 Playing area: goal keeper.

Equipment and Attire

The most important piece of equipment is the ball. It is usually made of leather, though rubber balls and balls of similar material are also used. For senior players, the ball is 690-710 millimetres in circumference and weighs 400-450 grams, the same as a football. Junior players use a smaller, lighter ball.

The playing uniform is undergoing some exciting changes. The traditional short, pleated skirt and plain-coloured polo shirt are giving way to body suits, soft-flowing skirts and bright shorts and shirts. The change emphasises colour and comfort and is proving very popular with the modern players. Many teams coordinate their warm-up track suits with their playing uniform.

Footwear has also changed, with a number of manufacturers developing netball shoes. Players should look for a shoe that cushions landing, provides solid heel and arch support, and is light, comfortable and durable.

As netball is basically a non-contact sport, the use of protective equipment for players is limited. It is common in some countries for players to tape ankles to reduce the risk of serious injury, or to use ankle guards for the same purpose. Some players use mouth guards as well. On the court, goalposts are often padded to reduce the risk of injury to players in case of collisions.

Fitness for Netball

To play netball requires speed and agility—the game constantly tests your reactions. You must maintain your speed for the duration of the game, so you need an endurance base. The demands of the game dictate the type of fitness work necessary to prepare you for competition. You should build your endurance base in the off-season. Do it with training that is interspersed with speed drills. For example, during a 20-minute run at an easy pace, incorporate a 15-second sprint every 5 minutes.

As the competitive season approaches, maintain one or two sessions per week for endurance; however, your fitness work should emphasise speed. Keep your work very court-specific. Remember, many of your moves will involve less than 10 strides, so use drills that work over short distances. Being the fastest player in 100 metres will not ensure you are first to the ball on court.

Designing effective and safe fitness programs requires expertise. Ask your coach or conditioning expert to design a program for you. Make sure that any outside expert you use understands the game. Then it is up to you, the athlete, to implement the program. Work diligently and look for long-term gains—these are the most beneficial.

The Warm-Up

Use the warm-up to begin the training session or before match play to prepare your body to cope with the demands you are about to place on it. You should be ready to work at game pace at the end of a warm-up. Netball demands rapid reactions, and your warm-up should reflect this. Your approach should be dynamic, using short bursts of speed. At the end of the 10- to 15-minute session, you should have raised a mild sweat and be ready to hit top speed from your first touch of the ball.

Begin the warm-up with dynamic running activities: forwards, backwards and sideways. Intersperse stretching between the running activities. Remember, muscles are stretched more effectively after you have warmed up a bit than when you are cold. Focus on stretching the large muscle groups: hamstrings, quadriceps, groin, calves, back, arms and shoulders. Stretch one muscle group between each run or drill. Then introduce the ball. Handle it quickly and surely, building your speed on the pass and speed of movement as you go. Begin with partner work and conclude with group work. Move quickly between activities while maintaining quality work.

In a 15-minute warm-up the running and stretching activities should take 10 minutes and the ball handling the final 5. You should take a few minutes' break at the end of the warm-up. Drink water and focus your thoughts on the task ahead in the final moments before the session begins.

The Cool-Down

All training sessions or matches should end with a cool-down. The cool-down has the opposite effect to the warm-up. Rather than preparing your body to work at top speed, the cool-down helps take your body from game tempo to a resting state. It is important to allow your heart rate to gradually slow down while still providing sufficient blood flow to aid recovery. The cool-down begins with gentle jogging activities followed by sustained stretching of the major muscle groups, and should take 10 to 15 minutes with three quarters of the time spent stretching.

STEP 1
CATCHING: SAFE AND SURE HANDS

In netball things happen quickly. This is no doubt due to the rule that says you can only handle the ball for three seconds. In that short space of time you have to catch the ball, control it, and make sure you send it safely on its way. In a single minute of play, you might have to do this three or four times. Over the course of a match, which is usually 60 minutes, you will handle the ball many times.

Catching is the first step in handling a netball, so it is appropriate that this is the first step to practice in becoming a netballer. It is important that you can catch the ball consistently. Good netballers let their fingers do the work. The fingers drive out to meet the ball, make contact and pull it in quickly.

In this chapter you'll learn the two kinds of catches in netball: the two-handed catch and the one-handed catch. The two-handed catch is the safest and allows for greater control, while the one-handed catch is less safe but gives you greater extension to the ball. You can reach just that bit further. In match play the correct choice of catch is crucial. When your opponent is closely contesting the ball, use *both* hands to catch. When you are soaring high, unopposed, use *one* hand.

As part of the catching skills we also introduce another important basic netball skill, the toss up, because it requires you to take possession of the ball extremely quickly. Umpires call for a toss up between two opposing players for numerous reasons: when the players have simultaneous possession; when both infringe; or when it is unclear just what has happened, such as when the ball has gone out of court and the umpire did not see who touched it last. Fast, sure hands win toss ups and possession of the ball.

Players sometimes think that basic skills like catching and winning a toss up are really not important; that it's clever tactics that win matches. Nothing could be further from the truth. It is absolutely essential to have the best basic skills you possibly can. Every session, to keep themselves sharp, the world's leading netballers practice drills for catching and winning toss ups.

Why Is Catching Important?

The rules of the game penalise a replayed ball (a ball you have caught and released—for whatever reason—then picked up again). If you have control of the ball and drop or fumble it, you cannot pick it up again until another player has handled it. In short, you have one chance to control the ball and if you mess up, that's it. The penalty for a replayed ball is a free pass for the opposition.

In a very close game, taking a really difficult catch or winning that vital toss up can give your team a winning edge. Make sure you work at these basic skills so your hands are safe and sure.

How to Catch

Begin with two hands. As your confidence and ability increase, practice the catch with one hand. You will probably find that you'll master the one-handed catch more easily with your dominant hand—that's natural—but make sure to work hard on catching with your non-dominant hand.

Whether you're catching with one hand or two, your body must be well-balanced and beginners should watch the ball all the way into their fingertips. To execute the two-handed catch, drive out both arms to take the catch as the ball approaches (see figure 1.1). With thumbs behind the ball and fingers outstretched, take the catch with the fingers. Pull the ball quickly into the chest while you prepare to make your pass. When catching with one hand, the fingers are extended fully as they drive out to take

FIGURE 1.1 **KEYS TO SUCCESS**

TWO-HANDED CATCH

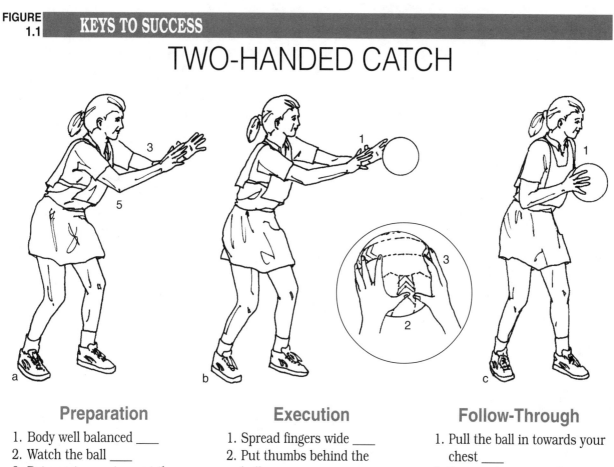

Preparation

1. Body well balanced ___
2. Watch the ball ___
3. Drive out arms to meet the ball ___
4. Extend arms and take the catch ___
5. Bend elbows slightly ___

Execution

1. Spread fingers wide ___
2. Put thumbs behind the ball ___
3. Firmly grip the ball with fingers ___

Follow-Through

1. Pull the ball in towards your chest ___
2. Prepare to pass or shoot ___

the pass (see figure 1.2). The ball is taken in the middle of the hand, with the fingers gripping it tightly. The wrist bends behind the ball to absorb the impact. Quickly pull the ball into the body using your other hand to protect it as you prepare to throw.

As you become more experienced you will be able to feel the catch come in while you scan the court for the best passing option. We call this an "automatic catch". When you can take the catch without having to watch the ball all the way into your fingertips, your catch is automatic. If you can consistently take an automatic catch without fumbling or dropping the ball, you should feel very pleased—you have safe hands.

FIGURE
1.2 **KEYS TO SUCCESS**

ONE-HANDED CATCH

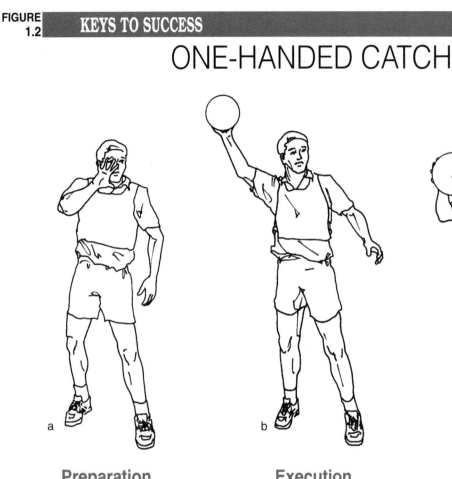

a

b

c

Preparation

1. Body well balanced ___
2. Watch the ball ___
3. Extend arm to ball ___

Execution

1. Move hand behind the ball ___
2. Bend wrist ___
3. Outstretch fingers ___
4. Firmly grip the ball with fingers ___
5. Balance ball on finger-tips ___

Follow-Through

1. Curve wrist and hand around ball ___
2. Pull ball into body ___
3. Use other hand to protect ball ___
4. Prepare to pass or shoot ___

How to Take the Toss Up

Stand facing your goal end and your opponent, 0.9 metres (3 feet) apart. Keep your arms straight, with hands to your sides. Balance your weight evenly, with the leg of your non-dominant side forward, its knee slightly bent, and your weight "down" (see figure 1.3).

Watch the ball in the umpire's hand. As the umpire steps between you to release the ball, get ready to react. You should feel like a tight spring ready to

be released. Make sure you do not move before the ball is released. If you do, you will be penalised and the opposing team will be awarded a free pass.

As the umpire releases the ball, swing both arms quickly forward and take possession as close to the point of release as possible. With a vice-like grip, pull the ball into your body. Remember to control your feet—don't overbalance. Widen your stance by repositioning your throwing-side foot sideways, then shift your weight to it for the throw.

FIGURE 1.3

TAKING THE TOSS UP

a

b

Preparation

1. Body balanced ___
2. Place non-dominant-side foot forward ___
3. Watch the ball ___
4. Keep arms straight by your sides ___
5. Umpire places ball in position ___

Execution

1. Umpire releases ball ___
2. Quickly raise arms ___
3. Put weight forward on the balls of your feet ___
4. Grab ball with fingers ___

c

Follow-Through

1. Pull ball in firmly ___
2. Keep weight down ___
3. Control feet, widen base ___

Alternative Method of Taking the Toss Up

An alternative action that players use quite successfully to win toss ups is called the "top-and-tail grip". As soon as the umpire releases the ball, shoot both hands forward. Position your throwing hand on top, reaching over the ball, and your other hand ready to grip the underneath (see figure 1.4). Once you have won possession, pull the ball quickly into your body. The fastest hands to the ball will win the toss up. If you are not gaining a lot of success when you swing the arms upwards, then try this alternate method.

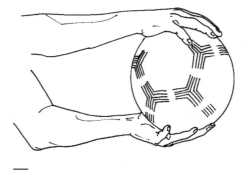

Figure 1.4   The top-and-tail grip.

CATCHING SUCCESS STOPPERS

Problems with your catch or toss up will be evident immediately: either you will drop or fumble the catch, or you will lose the toss up. Most errors are caused when players do not grip the ball correctly. Make sure your hands are well positioned on the ball, with thumbs behind it. Develop a vice-like grip; once the ball is in your hands it stays there. This will help you eliminate most of the problems with your catch.

Error	Correction
Catching	
1. You catch the ball with your palms.	1. Extend your fingers so they meet the ball.
2. You lose sight of the ball.	2. Watch the ball until you take the catch.
3. You don't protect the ball.	3. Pull the ball into your body once you have control of it.
4. You don't control the one-handed catch.	4. Use the two-handed catch until you become more proficient with one hand.
Toss Up	
1. You raise your hands before the ball is released.	1. Focus on the ball and listen for the whistle.
2. You overbalance as you move your arms.	2. Widen your base.

DRILLS

Safe, sure hands are best developed with individual practice. Devote five minutes of the day to work at your catch. Set yourself tasks that get progressively more difficult. Watch the ball throughout the practice. As your confidence and your ability increase, begin to practice the catch without looking at the ball all of the time. See if you can "feel" it happen.

1. Just Hands

Hold your hands loosely in front of your face. Quickly open your fingers and thumbs to the catch position until you cannot stretch them any farther, then close your hands. Open and close both hands quickly 10 times, then each hand separately 10 times.

Success Goal = 10 quick finger openers to the catching position ___

Success Check
- Thumbs should almost touch behind the "catch" ___
- Fully extend fingers ___
- Eyes watch your fingers ___

To Increase Difficulty
- Use the right hand only.
- Use the left hand only.
- Change the starting position of your hands. Try above the head, on the right side, low near the ground, and on the left side.
- Use both arms and fingers. Hold your arms loosely beside waist and extend both arms and fingers to the catching position. When using your arms, your target goal is 5.

2. Fast Hands

This drill is designed to speed the hands rather than to control the catch. Stand about a step away from a practice wall, facing it. With the ball in your right hand, bat it quickly against the wall, at shoulder height, allowing your fingertips to do the work. If you bat quickly, the ball rebounds back to your hand: that is, it maintains the same position on the wall. We say the ball is "staying on the wall" when this happens. If you tap the ball too slowly, the ball does not return to your hand; it falls down.

Success Goal = 10 consecutive taps with each hand ___

Success Check
- Fingers strike the ball ___
- Wrist and hand move quickly ___
- Ball maintains same position on the wall ___
- Eyes watch the ball ___

To Increase Difficulty
- Move ball up and down wall.
- Move ball across wall.
- Maintain the movement while you change hands.
- Reverse your starting position, putting your back to the wall. Turn your hand so it faces the wall and turn your head so you can see the ball.

To Decrease Difficulty
- Throw the ball and catch it one-handed until you establish the speed necessary for tapping.

BISHOP BURTON COLLEGE
LIBRARY

3. Stationary Catching

This drill provides stationary catching practice using a wall and a partner. Focus on the fundamentals of controlling the ball and developing safe hands.

a. Toss the ball into the air about one metre above your head. Extend both hands to the ball so that you take the catch quickly and cleanly. Pull the ball in, while at the same time bending your knees slightly.

b. Stand one metre from a practice wall. Throw the ball onto the wall and take the catch quickly and cleanly with both hands.

c. Have a partner stand a few metres in front of you. Your partner should begin by throwing the ball to you at chest height. Take the catch quickly and cleanly. As you become more skilful, have your partner speed up the pass. Your partner should vary the positioning and angle of passes to include high and low balls.

Success Goal = 10 consecutive catches for each variation ____

Success Check
- Eyes on the ball ____
- Fully extend your arms to take the ball ____
- Pull the ball in quickly after the catch ____

To Increase Difficulty
- Catch with one hand instead of two.
- Alternate one-handed catches between your right and left hands.

4. Double Catches

This is a partner drill intended to speed up the catch. Stand about two metres away from and facing your partner. You both have a ball. Put your feet about shoulder-width apart, and slightly bend your knees to lower your centre of gravity.

a. On the command "go", simultaneously pass the ball to each other, using two hands—you throw a straight pass, your partner throws a high pass. Both of you should take the catch quickly and immediately release the same pass. The ball should move quickly between you, with your wrists and fingers extending to catch, and then flicking to release.

b. Both players have their arms outstretched to the side with a ball balanced on the right hand. On "go", both of you release a one-handed straight pass to your partner's outstretched left hand. Quickly catch the ball with your left hand and then throw it back to your partner's right hand. You should throw and catch the balls simultaneously, with speed.

Success Goal = 20 total simultaneous passes between players without a drop

   a. 10 two-handed passes ____

   b. 10 one-handed passes ____

Success Check

- Spread fingers widely ____
- Balance ball on fingertips ____
- Flick ball with fingers and wrist ____

To Increase Difficulty

- Vary the pass: you use a high pass, your partner a low pass.
- Clap hands between each catch.
- Reverse your starting positions so you have your backs to each other. Turn around quickly on "go".
- Walk, then run while still controlling the ball. Can you reach top speed and still maintain speed on the ball?

To Decrease Difficulty

- Begin by passing one ball between your right hand and your partner's left hand. When you have achieved the success goal, introduce the second ball.

5. Steal Don't Touch

Stand beside your partner, facing the practice wall. You should stand three to four steps away from the wall, and about half a metre from your partner. Ask your partner to throw the ball hard onto the wall so it rebounds straight back to her or him. As the ball returns, you quickly reach across to catch the ball, using two hands, before your partner catches it. Your partner should try to beat you to the catch. Neither player should move their feet—let your hands do the work. To maintain your balance, bend your knees to lower your centre of gravity.

Success Goal = 5 consecutive catches without contacting your partner ___

Success Check
• Watch the ball ___
• Extend arms and fingers ___
• Grab the ball firmly ___
• Do not contact your partner ___

To Increase Difficulty
• Use one hand to take the catch.
• Vary the speed of the ball.
• Take the catch on the move. Start the drill two steps away from your partner.

6. Catching on the Move

When you feel that you have mastered the basic task of catching, begin to include drills that require you to move to the ball to take the catch. Here are three drills to try:

a. As you toss the ball high above your head, jump into the air using a two-foot take-off. Take the catch with both hands. Aim to have both your hands and your body at full extension before you pull the ball in.

b. Stand two metres from the wall. Throw the ball so that it bounces off the wall. Run in to take the catch before the ball falls to the ground.

c. Have a partner throw the ball for you to run and catch. Make sure that your partner places the ball into the space ahead of you so that you really have to extend yourself to take the catch.

Success Goal = 10 consecutive successful catches moving to the ball for each variation ___

Success Check
• Eyes on the ball ___
• Take the catch with arms at full extension ___
• Fingers meet the ball ___
• Wrists absorb the catch ___

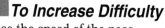

To Increase Difficulty
• Increase the speed of the pass.
• Vary the direction of the ball.
• Have your partner stand three metres in front of you and throw the ball for you to run and catch.

7. Take the Toss

Here are two drills to help increase your toss up speed. They can be easily slotted into training sessions, particularly after very demanding drills. Using an opponent gives you game-situation practice and increases interest in the drill.

a. Stand ready to take an imaginary toss up. Say "go" to yourself and see how quickly you can bring your hands up to where you catch the ball. This helps you to develop a fast reaction when the umpire introduces the ball.

b. Stand facing your partner, 0.9 metres (3 feet) apart, arms and hands by your sides, body still and tensed. In this position you are ready to react to the umpire's whistle, which signals the release of the ball. Quickly pull your arms and hands up to snatch the ball before your opponent has time to gain possession.

Success Goal =

a. 10 toss up actions as quickly as you can ____

b. First to win 3 consecutive toss-ups ____

Success Check

• Weight on balls of feet ____
• Knees bent ____
• Hands tensed at hips ____

To Increase Difficulty

• Play the best of 5 toss ups.
• Win one toss up then move to play a winner from another pair.

CATCHING SUCCESS SUMMARY

Catching is the first step to becoming a successful netball player. Ask someone trained in netball, your teacher, coach, or another trained observer or player, to evaluate your technique according to the checklist in figures 1.1 and 1.2. Focus on your preparation, execution, follow-through for both a two-handed and one-handed catch. Watch the ball all the way into your fingers when you begin catching. Your arms should drive forward to meet the ball, and pull it in quickly once you have possession. Use two hands at first, then one. This will allow you to reach just that little further to the ball. As your confidence grows and you hold the ball safely in your hands, you can begin to focus on the court play around you as you take the catch; it is now becoming automatic.

STEP

2 PASSING: THROWS TO KNOW

Because netballers do not have the option to dribble the ball, netball is very much a passing game. To move the ball up and down the court, team members throw it to each other using either one or two hands. This emphasis on passing is one of the factors that distinguishes netball from its game of origin, basketball, so it is not surprising that throwing skills have become highly specialised. Each of the leading nations has developed its game around the pass it considers to be most effective.

Australian players are often described as having bullet-like passing. Their philosophy to be fairly practical and straightforward: they consider the quickest route between one player and another to be a straight line. As often as they can they send a flat, hard, one-handed pass to each other. The speed generated, particularly by elite athletes, is awesome—it tests their catching skills to the limit. It has also been known to intimidate the opposition who frequently have no idea just where that pass came from.

The New Zealanders, on the other hand, have developed their game around the two-handed pass. They believe the player has more control over the ball when using both hands to throw. While the Kiwis tend to use more variety in their passes than the Australians, they have increased their use of higher velocity passing in recent years. In netball terms, we call high-velocity passing "putting speed on the ball".

England, the home of netball, developed its game around the high ball: a long floating pass which had a unique release and was delivered with pinpoint accuracy. The mastery of these one- or two-hand passes was England's early trademark. No other teams used the high ball as frequently or as well as England did. Their long-striding attacking play suited the lopping ball. However, it was not particularly successful against the power of Australia and

New Zealand because it gave the defenders far too much time to react. This has resulted in a major shift in England's approach to passing over recent years.

The most exciting netballers in the world, the West Indians, use a combination of approaches. One moment the ball is flying high overhead and the next it is down around your feet. You are never quite sure just where the ball will come from. Their flair and skill provide great excitement for the fans.

The purpose of this step is to introduce the basic passing techniques of the game. Of course it does not cover all possibilities, but it does provide you with the ability to play the game effectively. To be most successful, today's players should develop a repertoire of passes so that an element of surprise is always there. This chapter will help get you started.

There are three important parts of the skill of passing that the aspiring netballer needs to develop: (1) the technique of the various throws, (2) how to place a pass accurately, and (3) the ability to select the most appropriate throw in play. This step allows you to develop the techniques you need to be successful and provides some simple ways to develop accuracy. Selecting the appropriate pass is covered in later steps when we combine skills.

Why Is Passing Important?

To be able to play netball you need to pass the ball. To play successfully you have to pass the ball accurately. Each time you have possession of the ball on the netball court you will have to throw it, except if you are a shooter; then you will have to shoot as well.

Throwing is one of the most used skills in the game. No matter where you play, whether you are in the mid-court as centre, or on the goal line as goal defence, you have to pass the ball. In a netball game, your team will have passed the ball many times down court to your shooters. Netball teams that have good passing skills give their shooters many opportunities to score. The reverse is also true: poor passing skills restrict your team's opportunities and provide turnovers for your opponents to capitalise on.

When the ball is passed with pinpoint accuracy it is very difficult for your opponents to defend. In netball it is often said that teams that can thread the ball through the eye of a needle are unbeatable—a saying that most appropriately sums up the importance of accurate passing in this game.

Types of Passes

Netball throws fall into two categories: two-handed and one-handed passes. Within these categories are high ball and low ball passes. High ball passes travel overhead in an arc and include the lob, the shoulder pass, and the side pass. Low ball passes, such as the bullet pass, travel in a more direct line between the players. It is recommended that you become proficient with the basic two-handed and one-handed passing movements. The two-handed passes you're introduced to here include the chest pass, the bounce pass, the overhead pass, and the side pass. One-handed passes include the shoulder pass, the lob pass, the bullet pass, the underarm pass, and the bounce pass. The passes and their advantages are listed in table 2.1. Mastering these basic techniques will enable you to develop a versatile range of throws that will keep your opponents guessing.

If you are a very young player, you might find it easier to use a smaller ball and try two-handed passes first. You will find that using both hands gives you more power initially.

Two-Handed Passes

These are the easiest throws to begin with because you use both hands to execute the pass. Your hands sit either behind the ball or top-and-tail it (above and below). Your wrists and fingers guide the ball, and your elbows, arms and body weight generate speed and distance on the pass.

For the beginner this enables you to generate a good long throw, even though you may not have yet developed much upper body power. The more experienced netballer will find two-handed throws very useful because they are difficult for your opponent to anticipate early. When the ball is being held in two hands close to the chest it may be released as a chest pass, a bounce, or a high ball. This probably explains why the two-handed pass is frequently used to pass into the goal circle or at the centre pass.

The two-handed throw also has a built-in safety device: it can be retrieved quite easily at any point before the final release. The one-handed pass, on the other hand, is often difficult to retrieve once the throwing action has begun.

Table 2.1	Types of Passes and Their Advantages	
Type of Pass	**Method of Release**	**Advantages**
Chest	Two hands	Quick, accurate pass, long or short; easily controlled
Bounce	One or two hands	Short, low pass, great for confined spaces, particularly in goal circle
Overhead	Two hands	High, floating or straight pass; clears defenders' outstretched hands well
Side	Two hands	Quick, straight pass, easily controlled
Shoulder	One hand	Long, straight pass, covers distance well
Lob	One hand	Floating pass, long or short; pinpoint accuracy
Bullet	One hand	Fast, direct pass; accurate, used for short and medium distances
Underarm	One hand	Short, accurate pass that brings an element of surprise

Chest Pass

To execute the two-handed chest pass, hold the ball firmly with the fingertips of both hands. Place your thumbs behind the ball, wrists cocked. Hold the ball close to your chest, elbows to your sides. Your body weight should be evenly distributed between both feet, which are usually shoulder-width apart (see figure 2.1). Watch the receiver—you need to make quick decisions on the direction and speed of the ball before you release it. Train yourself to focus on the target. Flick the ball from your hands, using your wrists to initiate the pass and your fingers to direct the ball.

The ball can travel either in a straight line or an arc. Use your forearms and body weight to provide more power and distance. Follow through with your fingers, wrists and forearms.

The chest pass is commonly used to pass to a player who is in front of the defender. When the receiver is close, two or three metres away, you aim to place the ball into her or his fingertips. In this situation you release the two-handed chest pass with minimum pressure. When the receiver is some distance away you need to release a powerful ball.

FIGURE 2.1 **KEYS TO SUCCESS**

CHEST PASS

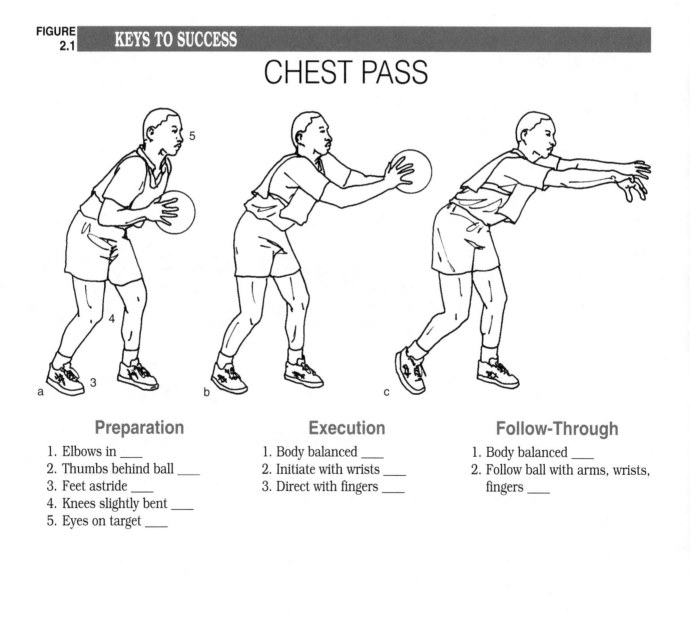

Preparation
1. Elbows in ___
2. Thumbs behind ball ___
3. Feet astride ___
4. Knees slightly bent ___
5. Eyes on target ___

Execution
1. Body balanced ___
2. Initiate with wrists ___
3. Direct with fingers ___

Follow-Through
1. Body balanced ___
2. Follow ball with arms, wrists, fingers ___

Bounce Pass: Two-Handed

Hold the ball firmly in the fingertips of both hands. If you want to release the ball in front of your body, then position your hands on top of the ball. For a sideways release, place your thumbs behind the ball so that they almost touch in the middle. The hand on the throwing side sits to the underside of the ball. The other hand sits toward the top side of the ball (see figure 2.2).

Flick your wrists and fingers to release the ball. Aim to have the ball bounce close, about a metre in front of the receiver to assist with the catch. You should aim for the receiver to take the ball at waist height or lower, remembering that high-rising balls are easy for the defender to intercept. Follow through with your arms, fingers and wrists, while relaxing your shoulders and bending your knees deeply to maintain body balance.

The rules of the game allow for only one bounce, and it is important that you bounce the ball wisely. The bounce pass allows an element of surprise—particularly when executed with two hands—because you can disguise it so well. It is frequently used in and around the goal circle as attackers endeavour to outwit defenders and pass safely to shooters.

FIGURE 2.2   **KEYS TO SUCCESS**

BOUNCE PASS

Preparation

1. Elbows in ___
2. Thumbs behind ball ___
3. Knees slightly bent ___
4. Eyes on target ___

Execution

1. Body balanced ___
2. Initiate with wrists ___
3. Direct with fingers ___

Follow-Through

1. Follow ball with arms and wrists ___
2. Relax shoulders ___
3. Knees stay bent ___

Overhead Pass

Hold the ball firmly in both hands, which are raised above your head. Make sure that your thumbs are behind the ball. Use your wrists and fingers to propel the ball either in a straight line or upwards to your target. Follow through with your fingers and wrists (see figure 2.3).

Figure 2.3 The two-handed overhead pass.

This pass is valuable when the opposition has a really strong defence on the ball. When you raise the ball above your head you make it easier to release safely. You have much better variety with this pass, a gentle, well-placed, short pass. You can also generate considerable power for a long pass.

Side Pass

Hold the ball to your side, close to your body, at about shoulder height. Hold the ball firmly with your fingertips and place your thumbs behind the ball; in fact they should almost touch in the middle of the ball. The hand on the throwing side sits to the underside of the ball; the other hand sits towards the top-side of the ball (see figure 2.4). Flick the ball with both wrists and fingers towards your target. Follow

through with your wrists and fingers. Use your body weight to increase power, and take your weight onto your front foot if court space permits.

Figure 2.4 The two-handed side pass.

You can use the side pass as a quick "flick on", or as a much longer pass. It is a very versatile pass, and therefore is used quite extensively, especially as a useful option at the throw in or centre pass.

One-Handed Passes

The one-handed pass is the power ball of the game. This is due more to the way the Australians have developed the throw than to a biomechanical analysis of the action. In netball today the hard, quick balls come from the one-handed throws.

To execute the one-handed pass, hold the ball with the outstretched fingers of your throwing hand and place your non-throwing hand on the ball to protect or steady it. Keep your body weight down in a balanced position, opposite foot to your throwing hand forward, and knees slightly bent. It's important to watch the target. In match play you have to make important decisions regarding the delivery of the pass to the selected target, so right from the beginning train yourself to focus on the receiver. As you release the ball and send it to your target, make sure your fingers guide the ball; your arms and shoulders provide the power and speed. Also be sure to release the ball close to your body.

To generate more power and distance, "open" your shoulder prior to releasing the ball. To do this, simply pull your arm and throwing hand back behind your body. This causes the torso to rotate slightly and the shoulder to open. To generate even more power, add body weight to the throw by stepping forward towards the target.

The use of the follow-through step must be selective. The rules of the game provide the thrower with a protected space, 0.9 metres (3 feet). Stepping forward can lessen the distance a defender must maintain, which can put the release of your throw under pressure.

Finally, follow through with your throwing hand and transfer your body weight from your back foot to your front foot. Do not infringe the Footwork Rule (see page 37).

Shoulder Pass

Begin with the ball on the fingertips of your throwing hand (see figure 2.5). Position your elbow at right angles to your shoulder. Hold the ball close to your body at shoulder height. Your hand is behind the ball and your elbow extends away from your body. Protect the ball with your non-throwing hand. Your opposite foot to the throwing hand should be forward and your shoulder open, ready for a distance

FIGURE 2.5 **KEYS TO SUCCESS**

SHOULDER PASS

Preparation	Execution	Follow-Through
1. Hand behind ball ___	1. Shoulder open ___	1. Follow ball with throwing hand ___
2. Ball on fingertips ___	2. Provide speed with arm and body ___	2. Move back foot through ___
3. Ball protected by non-throwing hand ___	3. Release non-throwing hand ___	3. Transfer weight forward ___
4. Weight down, knees slightly bent ___	4. Extend arm to help guide throw ___	
5. Opposite foot forward ___	5. Propel with wrist ___	
	6. Direct with fingers ___	
	7. Eyes on target ___	

pass. Release the ball from your fingers, follow through with your throwing hand, and transfer your weight forward as your back foot moves through.

The shoulder pass is the most commonly used one-handed pass. Use it whenever you need a quick, direct pass. It is frequently used at the centre pass, in the goal third, and by defenders who wish to send a long ball quickly out of their third.

Lob

This is the one-handed high ball that requires subtle finger control to direct the ball accurately to the target. Begin with the ball on the fingers of your throwing hand at shoulder height with your elbow bent at a right angle and your throwing hand under the ball (see figure 2.6). Your throwing hand should climb in

FIGURE 2.6 **KEYS TO SUCCESS**

LOB

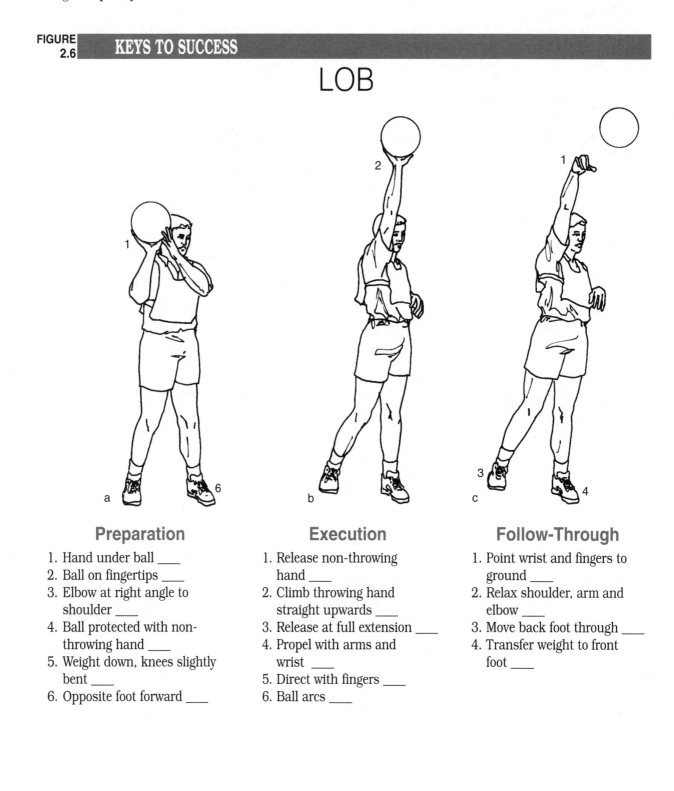

Preparation

1. Hand under ball ___
2. Ball on fingertips ___
3. Elbow at right angle to shoulder ___
4. Ball protected with non-throwing hand ___
5. Weight down, knees slightly bent ___
6. Opposite foot forward ___

Execution

1. Release non-throwing hand ___
2. Climb throwing hand straight upwards ___
3. Release at full extension ___
4. Propel with arms and wrist ___
5. Direct with fingers ___
6. Ball arcs ___

Follow-Through

1. Point wrist and fingers to ground ___
2. Relax shoulder, arm and elbow ___
3. Move back foot through ___
4. Transfer weight to front foot ___

a straight line to full extension, where you release the ball at full extension for maximum flight. Throw the ball in an arc to go over defenders, then follow through with your wrist and fingers.

The lob is often used at the throw-in. Players lead forward and then suddenly drive back calling for the lob to clear a congested area. Shooters who hold space in the goal circle also call for the lob to be delivered accurately to them. It is very hard for a defender to contest a well-placed lob without causing contact.

Bullet Pass

This is the powerful, waist-high ball that shoots through space. Begin with the ball on your throwing hand at waist level, and tuck your elbow into your waist (see figure 2.7). Protect the ball with your non-throwing hand. Place your feet about shoulder-width apart, with the foot of your non-throwing side forward. Slightly bend your knees and balance your body well. To start the release, quickly open your forearm and wrist. Whip your hand forward to propel the ball in a straight line to the target. Follow through with your throwing hand and back foot. Transfer your body weight forward to this foot.

Figure 2.7   Preparing the bullet pass.

The bullet pass is very effective when you need to move the ball quickly into a small space; for example,

throwing in from the sideline or passing into the goal circle.

Underarm Pass

The underarm pass can originate from any starting position, and is most effective when it has an element of surprise. Its most common use is by shooters who back-pass to gain a better shooting position.

Balance the ball on the outstretched fingertips of your throwing hand. Pull your arm quickly back in a circling action, similar to the warm-up action of a softball pitcher. Your elbow comes up and then back as the rotation occurs. Release the ball in a forward movement as your hand passes your thigh. Follow through with your fingers and wrist.

Bounce Pass: One-Handed

When you have mastered the two-handed bounce pass, try the one-handed version. This will give you a greater range of options to use the throw effectively. The one-handed bounce pass enables you to release the ball further from your body so that you can really reach out around defenders before you let the throw go. Make sure you keep your knees well bent to maintain good balance.

Begin with the ball in your throwing hand at waist height. Use your non-throwing hand to protect the ball. As you release your non-throwing hand, extend your throwing arm sideways. Pull your wrist back behind ball, then quickly release the ball with a downwards movement. Use your fingers to direct its path. Aim to have the ball bounce close, about a metre in front of the receiver, to assist with the catch. You should aim for your receiver to take the pass at waist height or lower.

Outsmarting Your Opponent: The Baulk

In a baulk the ball does not actually leave your hands, so it is not technically a pass. It is, however, a very useful ball skill to develop, and since it is used as a preliminary movement for a pass, it is appropriate to introduce it here.

The term baulk is, I believe, Australian. The English call the movement a "feint", while the Caribbeans refer to it as a "fake". Although netballers may use different terms to describe the action, the execution and intention are quite universal. The baulk is used as a surprise, to trick the defending players into reacting to what they think is a throw. It is very useful to create space for passing when defenders are pressuring the pass with their outstretched hands almost over your ball.

The baulk is done with two hands. Both hands are needed to ensure the ball does not leave your hands. If you tried to execute this skill with one hand, the ball would move and you would be penalized for replaying the ball.

To perform a baulk, hold the ball firmly with both hands and initiate a throwing action with both your forearm and wrist. Hold the ball tightly so that is not in fact released. Remember that replaying the ball incurs a penalty, so make sure that the ball does not leave your fingertips. Quickly recoil your hands and reposition to execute your selected pass.

If the baulk is successful, the defender should commit to what appears to be a pass, giving you room to execute your throw. Remember, you only have three seconds to handle the ball, so speed is important.

PASSING SUCCESS STOPPERS

The most common passing errors are caused by poor technique. If you have a technical problem, return to the basic throw procedure and work hard until you feel you can execute it automatically, without having to think about the detail of the movement. Gradually begin to add defensive pressure to the pass. Be confident. If your technique is sound, practice under pressure will be well rewarded. If you are making mistakes because you frequently use the wrong pass, it will be important for you to work in situations that constantly challenge your decision-making ability.

Error	Correction
1. Your throw lacks direction.	1. Check your release: are you using your fingers?
2. Your pass falls short.	2. Open your shoulder or put your body weight behind the throw.
3. Your two-handed pass drifts.	3. Grip the ball tightly with both hands. One hand is dominating, causing the ball to veer.
4. Your throw is dropped by your team-mate.	4. Ease off the power; you might be propelling the ball too hard.
5. Your opponent intercepts your pass.	5. Check your release and your footwork; you might be taking the ball out near your opponent or stepping forward and lessening the distance between you.

PASSING

DRILLS

1. Passing Warm-Up

Here are a few warm-up activities you can do before you start each practice. These will help you develop a good feel for the ball.

a. Throw the ball from one hand to the other across the body. Now try it above the head.

b. Throw and catch the ball to yourself. Use two hands and then use one hand. Throw the ball above your head, behind your back so you have to turn to catch it, to your right side, and to your left side. Now clap before you catch it.

c. With your feet astride, place the ball between your knees, with one hand to the back of ball and the other hand to the front. Change hands without allowing the ball to fall to the ground.

d. With a ball in each hand, throw and catch them simultaneously, first with the same hand, then with the opposite hand.

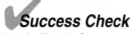

Success Goal =

a. 5 successful passes with each variation ___

b. 10 successful passes with each variation ___

c. 10 successful changes without dropping the ball ___

d. 5 successful passes with each variation ___

Success Check

• Grip ball with fingers ___

• Propel ball with arms and wrists ___

• Guide flight with fingers ___

• Release ball quickly ___

2. Target Ball

Target ball is a versatile drill to help develop your aim using a variety of target locations, distances, and passes. Remember to practice proper form with your release and follow-through.

a. Draw five hands at various heights on a wall with a piece of chalk. Take three steps from the wall to begin your practice. Using a shoulder pass, see how many throws it takes to hit every hand in order once. Now use the two-handed chest pass and repeat the exercise.

b. Mark five chalk lines on the ground at varying distances from the wall. Try to hit one target with one pass from each line. Then try to hit all targets from each line. When you have achieved your success goal, choose another pass and begin the drill again.

c. Use targets on the ground for high ball practice. Mark three to four large crosses on the ground. Release the ball high above your head and see if it can land on the targeted cross. Use both the one-handed and two-handed passes when practicing.

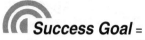

Success Goal =

a. 5 passes to targets from 5 throws ___
b. 5 passes to each target from 5 throws at different lines; 5 passes to all targets from 5 throws ___
c. 3 passes to targets from 3 throws ___

✔ Success Check

• Guide the ball with fingers ___
• Open shoulder before release ___
• Follow through with fingers, wrists and body ___

To Increase Difficulty

• Change hands and try passing with the other hand.
• Increase, by two, the number of steps you take from the wall to begin the practice. Once you are out at 10 to 12 steps you are handling a good long ball.
• Use other throws: the chest pass, the bullet pass, the two-handed overhead, and the underarm. Always begin close to the wall and achieve your goal before increasing the difficulty by stepping back.
• Now repeat the drills from the reverse position. Start the practice with your back to the wall. Throw the ball into the air above your head. Jump to catch it and turn to face the wall as you land. Make sure that you achieve your success goal at each activity before you move on. If you work hard you will find there is no noticeable difference in the speed and accuracy of the pass from a front start and a reverse start.

To Decrease Difficulty

• Use one target and gradually add others when you master the technique.

3. Hit the Bin

Stand four to five large strides away from a waste paper basket that can hold your netball. You are facing away from the target—the bin—holding the ball. Pivot quickly to face the bin and release a lob. Aim to have the pass land in the bin. Run quickly to retrieve the ball. Return to your starting position and release a bounce pass to hit the bin.

Success Goal = 6 successful passes that hit the bin ___

Success Check
• Guide ball with fingers ___
• Lob arcs to bin ___
• Bounce travels low ___

To Increase Difficulty
• Use the two-handed overhead pass and the one-handed bounce pass.
• Increase the distance by two strides. Alternate the lob and the two-handed overhead pass.
• Place a partner between yourself and the bin. Have your partner try to intercept your pass.

To Decrease Difficulty
• Reduce the success goal to 3 passes and use one throw. Start with the bounce pass. When you have achieved your goal, try the lob.

4. Hit the Hand

Stand three to four steps away from your partner. Have your partner raise a hand to full extension. Throw the ball to your partner's outstretched hand. If the ball is placed accurately your partner should not have to move at all to take the catch. Ask your partner to choose another position. Throw the ball to this target.

Success Goal = 5 consecutive passes to your partner's outstretched hand ___

Success Check
• Ball travels quickly to target ___
• Follow through with throwing hand ___
• Move weight onto front foot after release ___

To Increase Difficulty
• Increase the distance between you and your partner.
• Practice different throws
• Begin with your back to your partner. Throw and catch the ball, turn, and throw.
• Have your partner move to take the ball.
• Try to complete 5 different passes where both you and your partner are moving. Increase this to 10 successful passes.

BISHOP BURTON COLLEGE
LIBRARY

5. Pick-Up

This is a good activity to practise movement to the ball and a quick release. Stand four metres away from your partner, who has the ball. Have your partner roll the ball quickly towards you. Once the ball is released, run to pick it up. Use a two-handed chest pass to return the ball to your partner's outstretched hands.

Success Goal = 5 successful consecutive pick-ups and return passes ___

Success Check
- Move quickly to the ball ___
- Pick ball up cleanly ___
- Focus on target ___
- Release pass and follow through ___

To Increase Difficulty
- Use the overhead pass to return.
- Have your partner throw the ball along the ground.
- Increase the distance another metre.

To Decrease Difficulty
- Have your partner place the ball on the ground.

6. Up and Back

Stand five metres in front of your partner. Have your partner sprint towards you. When your partner is about one metre from you, have her or him stop quickly and sprint away from you. As this happens you release a lob. If the ball is well placed, it will be easy for your partner to jump into the air and take the catch at full stretch.

Success Goal = 3 well-placed lobs from 3 passes ___

Success Check
- Watch your target ___
- Body is well balanced ___
- Ball travels in a high arc ___
- Ball is well placed for receiver ___

To Increase Difficulty
- Use the two-handed overhead pass.
- Introduce a defender to contest the high ball.

To Decrease Difficulty
- Have your partner start one metre away and run slowly away from you.

7. Hands Over the Pass

The final test for throwing is to see if you can maintain accuracy when the pass is being pressured. Go back to the target practice on the wall. Start about five steps out. Throw the ball to yourself to begin the drill. As you catch, have your partner take up a position 0.9 metres (3 feet) directly in front of you and reach forward to pressure the ball. Throw the ball accurately to your target on the wall. When the defender's hands are over the ball, make sure you do not contact them. This is a good time to practice the baulk (feint).

Success Goal = 3 successful pressured passes to the target ____

Success Check
• Eyes on the target ____
• Aware of defender's hands ____
• Choose appropriate pass ____
• Shorten follow-through ____

To Increase Difficulty
• Use a third player to provide a stationary target by raising her or his catching hand.
• Have the third player provide a moving target for the pass.

8. Baulk and Pass

Stand five to six metres away from your partner. A defender is 0.9 metres (3 feet) directly in front of you with his or her hands stretched out over the ball. Your partner makes an attacking move. Use a baulk to clear the defender's hands before you pass to your partner.

Success Goal = 3 successful passes after a baulk ___

Success Check
- Baulk is quick and convincing ___
- Grip ball tightly for baulk ___
- Eyes on target ___
- Release ball quickly when opening is created ___

To Increase Difficulty
- Introduce a second attacking player. You must now select the best option from the two moves being made, then deliver the pass accurately.

PASSING SUCCESS SUMMARY

You have just tackled one of the game's major skills, passing. If you can execute a one-handed and a two-handed pass accurately, you are well on the way to becoming a good player. Test yourself on some of the passes by asking an instructor or practice partner to evaluate your passing skills according to the Keys to Success checklist in figures 2.1, 2.2, 2.5, and 2.6. Have you noticed how much more difficult it is to place the ball just right once you begin to move? As you become more confident in your throwing ability, increase the amount of practice you do on the move. Then begin to introduce some pressure over the pass. Keep trying to master a wide variety of throws to add depth to your game.

STEP 3

FOOTWORK: QUICK AND CONTROLLED

We have already looked at the importance of the basic work that hands do in netball: catching and throwing. Another basic element of the game involves the feet. If you are to master this exciting game, getting your feet under control is essential.

The Footwork Rules of netball are quite unique and specific, and in these modern times, somewhat controversial. Simply put, the rules state that after taking possession of the ball, the first grounded foot may not be re-grounded before the player releases the ball. An infringement of the Footwork Rule incurs a free pass for your opponents. This rule is further explained later in this chapter.

Originally the one-step rule was no doubt designed to cater to a genteel, ladylike way of playing. It is quite likely that ladies of Madame Osterberg's College of Physical Training at Hampstead felt it inappropriate for women to run the whole length of the court dribbling the ball. Restricting the movement to one step forced players to pass.

If the game had perhaps appealed only to the genteel, then the modern-day concerns would probably not have arisen. Today, however, the game is played by finely tuned athletes, many of whom undertake vigorous training schedules to seek international supremacy. Speed of movement has become a trademark of the leading nations' styles of play. The rapid acceleration and sudden stopping characteristic of today's game has caused questions to be asked regarding the link between the Footwork Rule and knee injuries. While there is no conclusive evidence to date that has led to a re-thinking of the rules, the discussion has brought about an intense review of coaching methods. There is now a much stronger emphasis on correct landing techniques and on footwork in general. Young players can feel confident that getting their feet under control can be done safely.

Why Is Footwork Important?

In a quick-moving, non-contact game like netball, being able to control your body is an important component of on-court success. The key to sound body control is good footwork. If your feet are under control, guiding your movement, keeping your body well-balanced, and allowing you to change speed and direction effectively, then you can concentrate on the important on-court decisions to make with the ball—the crucial matters that win or lose games. Players who fail to control their feet have difficulty progressing further, and they also incur penalties.

General Footwork Skills

To be a successful netball player you need to master the basic footwork skills of the game. Whether you are in attack or defence, you need a powerful take-off; to be able to run fast, change direction swiftly, and jump strongly; and the ability to sidestep. Mastering these important skills enables you to move with speed and agility—two key components of all our great players' games.

Take-Off

The first two steps of your planned movement to the ball are crucial. If you generate a powerful take-off your opponents find it very difficult to stay with you, and your chances of a successful catch are greatly enhanced.

A powerful take-off involves the whole body and initiates from a low base. Your weight should be down and your knees bent. Make sure that you drive with your arms and legs, and that your first step is forward. It is very common to see players begin their movements with a backward step or a few small steps that tend to go up and down on the spot, taking them nowhere and making it very easy for their opponent to defend.

You should practice the take-off from a starting position that has one foot in front of the other, and then repeat from a starting position where feet are astride. You will then be able to create a strong take-off from either starting position.

Running

When you are in a hurry on the netball court, you run. Having a powerful take-off gives you a decided edge. Being able to run well enables you to hold that advantage. You generate more power when you run using your arms as well as your legs. It is surprising the number of players who forget to use their arms to help them to run faster.

Although most of the running you do is forwards to meet the ball, make sure you can also run backwards. Players often lose their balance when running backwards. If you widen your stride and keep your body upright but knees bent, you should generate speed and avoid falling over.

Changing Direction

An ability to make frequent changes of direction on the netball court keeps the opposition guessing. They are never quite sure just what you are going to do next, and that is the way you like it.

Changes of direction should happen quickly, with an element of surprise. From your running stance, quickly lower your body weight at the same time that you plant your outside foot (the foot opposite the direction you intend to go). Absorb your body weight with this foot and then quickly push off in the opposite direction. The lower your body weight, the more powerful and more rapid the movement is.

Sidestep

Use the sidestep, or shufflestep, to move across a short space when you don't really have the time or the space to run. Your feet are astride with your weight down and knees bent. If you are to sidestep to the right, use your left leg to push off while your right leg widens the base by about half a stride. Then transfer your body weight to your right foot while your left foot moves a similar distance to the right. Keep your elbows raised at waist level to counterbalance the movement from the feet.

The sidestep is a quick, shuffling movement that again should be worked from a low base to generate a powerful movement. You can do a sidestep in all directions: sideways, backwards and forwards.

Jumping

To dominate aerial play you need to be able to jump strongly to take the ball. Good technique assists you to gain maximum extension to the ball. A jump from a stationary start is easiest to control.

The power of the jump originates in the legs. Begin a jump with a deep knee bend to initiate a strong movement. Use your arms to assist in the upward driving movement. Keep your body well balanced as you accelerate upwards.

You can generate even more height on your jump if you use a running start. Remember the important points of take-off when you combine the jump with a running movement: a two-foot take-off gives you more control in the air; a one-foot take-off and climb gives you better elevation.

How to Land

Poor landing technique means that your body has an unstable base from which to execute skills. It also increases the chance for injury. Netball demands rapid reactions to on-court action; good landing technique enables you to be in a well-balanced position and ready to respond instantaneously.

For the safest landing, you need to absorb the impact as effectively as you can. Two-foot landings cushion the impact more evenly than one-foot landings, so use a two-foot landing as often as possible. Allow your knees to bend and absorb some of the force. When you are running, particularly at top speed, you are traveling in a mainly horizontal way. Try to take a small jump immediately before you land. This will help you land in a more controlled vertical way so the knees and ankles can absorb the impact downward, not sideways. Of course, when you are running hard to take the ball you are not able to jump to the height you could achieve if you simply went straight up in the air for a spectacular high pass. To land safely, use two feet, bend the knees, and avoid turning or twisting movements.

There are occasions on court when you are simply not able to use both feet to land and must use a one-foot landing. The principle for executing the one-foot landing is the same. Try to jump a little higher than you would if you were using two-feet and allow your knee to bend more deeply on landing. Avoid twisting or turning movements. Bring your other foot into contact with the ground as soon as practical. This allows you to redistribute your body weight evenly.

Understanding the Footwork Rule

Once you have successfully landed, the Footwork Rule dictates your next move. The rule states that you cannot re-ground the first landed foot. While you have possession of the ball you may not drag or slide your landed foot, or hop on either foot.

The foot that touches the ground first after you catch the ball is the landed foot. It is important that you are aware of which foot you landed on. If you have landed on one foot, this is not a difficult task. When you use a two-foot landing, you can select which foot you want to use as the landed foot. You may then step with either foot, but you must throw the ball or shoot before re-grounding the landed foot.

Once you land with the ball, you need to pass or shoot within three seconds. While the important thing to remember is not to re-ground your landed foot, there is a wide range of foot movements you can use before you pass or shoot. You can

- pivot,
- pivot and step onto the other foot,
- jump,
- jump and turn in the air,
- step onto the other foot,
- step onto the other foot and jump, or

- step onto the other foot, then bring the first leg through, making sure you release the ball before the landed foot is re-grounded.

In short, the choice you have ranges from taking no step and simply pivoting, to fully extending the Rule and almost taking two steps. Isn't that a complex task? Elite players can do all this and more.

Choosing just when to do what takes much practice. To begin, apply the Rule with the basic techniques of pivoting and stepping-on, then build your repertoire. Remember you have only three seconds to handle the ball, so your feet need to work swiftly and surely.

How to Execute the Pivot

There will be many times when you take the ball facing in one direction and want to pass facing another. The pivot enables you to turn quickly on court (see figure 3.1). Having landed on two feet, select the appropriate side to turn: left or right. Keep your weight down, knees bent, and pivot to that side so you turn to face the opposite direction. Pivot on the ball of the landed foot by pushing off with the opposite foot. Follow through with the foot you used to push off with to regain a well-balanced position. You may step as many times as you wish with he opposite or pushing foot, to pivot and re-pivot if necessary. You are now facing your team's goal end and are ready to pass to a team member.

If you land on one foot, simply use it as your pivot foot. Turn in the direction you wish to go and bring the other foot through to keep your body balanced.

Remember the golden rule for pivoting: If you are rotating to the right, pivot on the right foot; if you are rotating to the left, pivot on the left foot.

FIGURE
3.1 KEYS TO SUCCESS

PIVOTING

a   b 5   c 1

Preparation

1. Take catch ___
2. Knees bent to cushion landing ___
3. Body balanced ___
4. Be aware of landed foot ___

Execution

1. Keep weight down ___
2. Keep body upright ___
3. Rotate body ___
4. Push body around with other foot ___
5. Spin on ball of pivot foot ___

Follow-Through

1. Reposition opposite foot ___
2. Keep body balanced ___
3. Eyes on target, prepare to pass ___

How to Execute the Step-On

You need to exercise sound judgment to use the Footwork Rule to your advantage. The step-on is an advanced skill, so don't rush into it or you might make mistakes. Make sure you have mastered the land and pivot before you try the step-on. It is best to use the step-on when you have outrun your opponent and no one is in front of you to offer a defensive move. The path is open and you step-on into it before you release your pass.

Having landed on one foot, step forward onto the opposite foot, then follow through with the landed foot (see figure 3.2). Release the ball before you re-ground the landed foot. If you use a two-foot landing, you can step forward onto either foot and then release the ball before the other foot is re-grounded. If you need to turn to face the opposite direction before you take the step, simply pivot on the landed foot, then step on.

Right-handed throwers should seek to land on their right foot. This allows them to step onto their left foot and be in a well-balanced position before executing the pass. For left-handed throwers, the reverse applies.

If you keep your body well balanced, you will be able to deliver your pass accurately. Remember that you might be moving very fast and you can use this speed, along with the stepping-on movement, to produce a powerful, long ball. If, however, the pass requires a fine touch, jump slightly when stepping on and use a two-handed throw.

FIGURE 3.2 **KEYS TO SUCCESS**

STEPPING ON

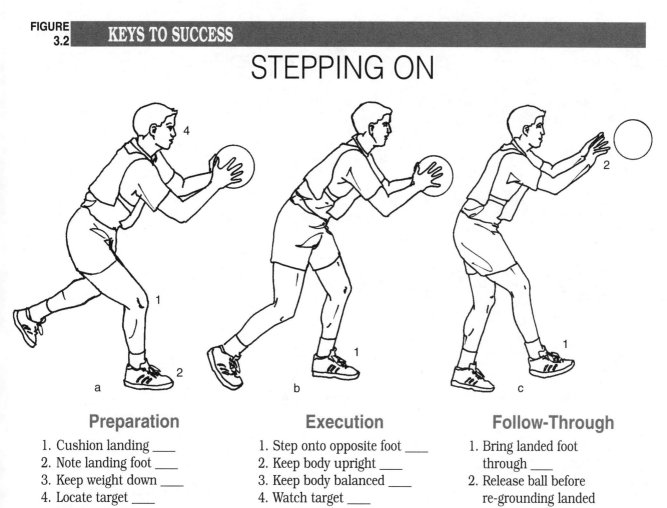

a	b	c

Preparation	**Execution**	**Follow-Through**
1. Cushion landing ____ 2. Note landing foot ____ 3. Keep weight down ____ 4. Locate target ____ 5. Keep momentum moving forward ____	1. Step onto opposite foot ____ 2. Keep body upright ____ 3. Keep body balanced ____ 4. Watch target ____	1. Bring landed foot through ____ 2. Release ball before re-grounding landed foot ____

Recovery Step

Use this step to quickly clear the space between you and your opponent after you have made an unsuccessful attempt to defend the pass. The rules of the game require a defending player to stand a distance of 0.9 metres (3 feet) from the landed foot of the attacker. The recovery step allows you to reassert yourself and pressure the pass or a shot because you are now in a "legal" position to re-enter play.

The recovery step is a backwards jump that takes you the required distance from the thrower; you land facing your opponent so that you can offer some defence on the ball (see figure 3.3). As your opponent takes the pass, stop your forward movement, drop your body low, knees well bent, push back from both feet, and jump backwards to the legal distance of 0.9 metres (3 feet). Now, quickly raise your arms and pressure the ball. Reach forward and target the point of release. Younger players should be taught to use both feet to jump back for the recovery step. Older players who have reasonable leg strength can jump back from one foot if needed.

FIGURE 3.3 — KEYS TO SUCCESS

RECOVERY STEP

Preparation

1. Stop movement ___
2. Recoil body ___
3. Move body weight down ___
4. Focus on opponent ___
5. Note opponent's landed foot ___
6. Watch the ball ___

Execution

1. Push off from both feet ___
2. Jump backwards strongly ___
3. Land 0.9 metres (3 feet) in front of opponent ___
4. Raise arms to pressure pass ___

Follow-Through

1. Try to intercept ball on release ___
2. If unsuccessful, drop arms ___
3. Keep weight down and defend opponent ___

FOOTWORK SKILLS SUCCESS STOPPERS

Running, landing, pivoting and stepping-on form the basic movements for footwork skills. You can easily add a simple jump to these. Young players often find footwork difficult to master, and it is very common for their modified rules to allow them to shuffle on the spot before they release the ball. This is a very sensible way to start. The older players need to check their footwork movements regularly to ensure that their feet are under control and are generating powerful body movements. Ask your coach to check your action to ensure you are not penalised for stepping or dragging your feet.

Error	Correction
General Footwork Skills	
1. Your first take-off step is backwards.	1. Use your arms to drive yourself forward.
2. Not enough speed on take-off.	2. Bounce quickly a few times on the spot before you drop your weight down and take off.
3. Not enough elevation on your jump.	3. Separate the running movement by pausing momentarily before take-off. Use a deeper knee bend at take-off.
4. Your upper body sways when you run.	4. Accentuate arm movement. Hold a stick or relay baton as you practice your running to help see just what your arms and hands are doing.
5. You lose balance when executing the sidestep.	5. Keep your body moving over the base created by the feet. As the outside foot reaches to extend the base, realign the upper body.
Landing	
1. Your body jerks when landing.	1. Use a deep knee bend to cushion the impact.
2. You overbalance when landing.	2. Widen your base and bend your knees.
3. You twist when landing.	3. Jump slightly before you land; it allows you time to realign your body before impact.
Pivoting	
1. You lose balance as you turn.	1. Keep your body upright and weight down.
2. Your landed foot lifts.	2. Keep your knees bent and weight down.
Stepping On	
1. You lose balance as you step on.	1. Check your stride length; you are most likely overstriding.
2. Your landed foot drags.	2. Keep well balanced and weight down on feet.
3. Your landed foot re-grounds.	3. Speed up the release of the ball.

Error	Correction
Recovery Step	
1. You are penalised for obstruction.	1. Your distance is too short—jump back farther. Practice jumping back with a stick on the ground that measures 0.9 metres (3 feet) so you become very familiar with the legal distance. Also, you might have raised your arms before you cleared the legal distance. Make sure you practice landing before you raise your arms.

FOOTWORK

DRILLS

Footwork skills are best practised frequently and in short bursts. Look for quality of movement rather than quantity. This means that in a practice session you should include only two or three patterns, and spend only one or two minutes on each movement.

Begin with a simple action and increase its difficulty as your confidence and ability grow. The work in this chapter is an area where you are able to create your own drills, so don't be afraid to use your imagination.

1. Take-Off Three Step

This drill allows you to work on your take-off skills. Focus on keeping your weight down and your movements explosive.

a. Jog the length of the court, 30.5 metres (100 feet). In each third say "go" to yourself, then take three powerful running steps. Aim to be at full speed in three steps.

b. Place a cone four metres in front of you. Jog forward. As you get close to the cone call "go" and practice your powerful take-off without contacting the cone. Use the running take-off first and then introduce the jump. Make sure you don't lose power now that there is an obstacle to think about.

Success Goal = 3 powerful take-off movements ___

Success Check
• Weight down on take-off ___
• Legs and arms driving ___
• Eyes up ___

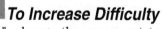**To Increase Difficulty**
• On "go", change the movement to a powerful jump; 2 running steps and a strong jump; 2 steps right, then a change of direction; 2 steps right, take an imaginary catch, land and pivot, 3 backward running steps.

2. Moving Your Feet Around the Triangle

Draw three crosses on the ground, five metres apart, to form a triangle. Stand at the first cross. On "go", sprint to the second cross. When you reach it, drop your weight, change direction, and without losing speed, sprint to the third cross where you execute a two-foot landing. Now turn around and repeat the exercise to return to the start.

Success Goal = Work the triangle 3 times: 6 changes of direction and 6 two-foot landings ___

Success Check
• Drive sprint with arms and legs ___
• Keep your head up watching play ___
• Anchor outside foot to effect change ___
• Bend knees to cushion the landing ___

To Increase Difficulty
• Use the one-foot landing in place of the two-foot landing.
• Sidestep to the second cross then execute as before.
• Run to the second cross and execute a recovery step, then back shuffle to the third cross. Turn and repeat the drill to return to the start.
• Place a cone on each of the crosses. Repeat the drills making sure that you can execute the movements without contacting the cone.

3. Leaping Around the Line

This drill helps you develop powerful elevation and gives you a chance to practice safe, controlled landings.

a. Stand on the sideline of the court. Leap from the left foot and land on the right foot. Bring the left foot through so that your body is well balanced. Repeat, leaping from the right foot.
b. Stand astride a sideline, facing the court, feet shoulder-width apart. Take a deep knee-bend position and jump as high as you can into the air. Bend knees to absorb the landing. Attempt to land back on the line and not to travel in the air.

Success Goal =
a. 6 strong leaps with a safe landing: 3 to the right and 3 to the left ___
b. 4 consecutive high jumps landing back on the line___

Success Check
• Keep body upright ___
• Drive movement with arms and legs ___
• Leap high ___
• Bend ankles and knees to land ___
• Maintain body balance ___
• Keep head up watching play ___

To Increase Difficulty
• Clap your hands 5 times above your head before you land.
• Scissors-kick your legs twice before you land.
• Try the same leaps, only this time with a short take-off of three or four running steps.
• Introduce the ball. Have a partner throw a ball and leap and catch it as you land.
• Now add a pivot to the run, leap and land. Once you have landed, pivot to face the opposite direction. When you can do this without the ball, include a catch and throw to the drill.
• Try the step-on instead of the pivot. When you land, take your full step forward and begin the next step before you release your pass.

4. Footwork Cone Circuit

This is best done in the goal circle, but it can be adapted to other court areas. Place a cone one metre in front of the goalpost. This is the central cone. Starting from the baseline, place four cones along the edge of the circle. Begin the drill by standing next to the central cone. Run to the first cone, change direction, and return to the central cone. Run to the second cone and return. Repeat this until you complete a circuit of all four cones.

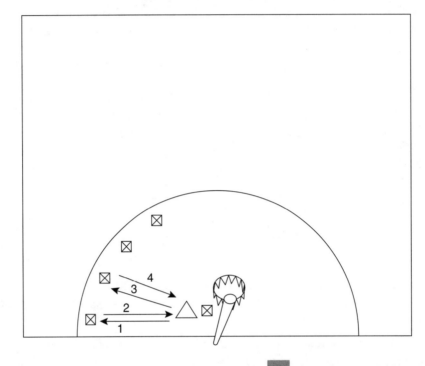

Success Goal = Move quickly between all five cones without touching them ___

Success Check

• Keep head up watching the play ___
• Move with speed ___
• Maintain body balance throughout ___

To Increase Difficulty

• Run to the outside cone, use a recovery step, and back shuffle to return to the central cone.
• Run to the outside cone. Jump and execute a two-foot landing before running backward to the central cone.
• Sidestep out and back to each cone.
• Have a partner start the drill after you reach the first outside cone. Maintain or increase this distance from your partner as you work through the cones. Your partner tries to catch you.

5. Recovery Step Practice

Mark a chalk line 0.9 metres (3 feet) from the transverse line. You are in a crouched position with one foot forward on the transverse line and the other a little more than shoulder-width behind. Make sure your weight is down. You should feel like a tight spring ready to uncoil. Push back strongly with both feet and jump back to clear the legal distance. If you have landed on the line your judgement is just right. As soon as you land, raise your hands to pressure the pass.

Success Goal = 5 successful recovery jumps to the legal distance; 0.9 metre line ____

Success Check

- Move weight down to start ____
- Push off strongly ____
- Clear distance 0.9 metres (3 feet) ____
- Raise body and hands up after landing ____

To Increase Difficulty

- Try the same recovery action but start by running three or four steps to the transverse line.
- Have your partner stand on the transverse line with a ball. When you have executed the recovery step, your partner releases the ball and you try to intercept it.
- Stand beside your partner on the transverse line. Toss the ball in the air. Both contest the catch. When you are unsuccessful, use the recovery step to defend the pass.

FOOTWORK SUCCESS SUMMARY

You have now mastered the basic foundations of movement on the netball court. Running, landing, pivoting, stepping and elevating all assist you in your attacking play, while the recovery step and the sidestep make you a very valuable defender. Be patient with your footwork. Give your feet quality practice time. If you build very solid foundations you will not have to return later to correct basic mistakes. Make sure you ask your coach or teacher to check your progress regularly according to the Keys to Success illustrated in figures 3.1 through 3.3. If you have a club umpire, ask him or her to watch your footwork too. They are, after all, the ones who make the on-court judgments.

STEP

4 SHOOTING: AIMING HIGH

Now we are going to look at a specialist skill of netball: shooting. Not all players want to be shooters, so before you decide what position to specialise in, try them all. This chapter will help you master the basics of this important and challenging skill.

Netball has a unique shooting style: the ball is released high and is usually released while the shooter is stationary. The shot has changed over time from a two-handed throw to the high release, one-handed shot used today. Early shooting actions released the ball low, which produced a very flat shot. When defenders began to intercept the ball on its way to the ring, shooting techniques were revised. England's Judy Heath was the first shooter to remove the downward pull from her action and use a technique that flicked the ball from her fingers and used her legs to generate power. Her accuracy almost enabled England to take the world crown in Jamaica in 1973.

In netball today, two basic shots are used. They have been developed by two of the game's great legends.

Australian superstar Margaret Caldow devised the high release technique that her country's shooters are now known for. Like Heath, Caldow's style of shot is based on a strong wrist action with very little down pull. The ball is held high above the head and travels in a high arc to the ring. Caldow was renowned for her ability to place the ball through the ring cleanly; rarely did her shot touch the side.

While individuals tend to modify the technique to suit their personal style, generally the principles developed by Caldow govern the approach to shooting today. Caldow is the only netballer to have played in three winning world championship teams. A fast-moving player, her court craft and her accuracy were telling factors in the Australian team's domination of the world stage from her first appearance in 1963 until her retirement in 1979.

Appearing on the world stage at a similar time to Caldow was the great Trinidadian shooter, Jean Pierre. She is one of a very few players who have competed in five consecutive World Championships. She played a major role in Trinidad and Tobago's success in the 1979 series. Her technique is used extensively by the Caribbean nations and players from North America. While Pierre's shot starts lower than Caldow's, her shooting arm climbs to a similar point of release. The main difference is in her foot placement. Pierre's shot has a front and back foot action, while Caldow's has the feet parallel.

The Australian high release shot and the Caribbean shot are the most successful shooting techniques in netball. Developed by players who lived in very different parts of the world, it is surprising the similarities exist. Try both actions before you decide which is the most appropriate for you; that way you will make an informed decision based on your experience.

Why Is Shooting Important?

There are only two players on a netball team who can shoot goals: the goal shooter and the goal attack. All of the team's scoring comes from these two positions, so you can see how important it is that players who wear these letters can shoot accurately.

When the ball comes into the shooter's hand the entire court focuses on the outcome. Being a shooter is not only a very responsible position, it is very appealing because of the focus these players get throughout the match.

How to Execute the Australian High Release

Shooters feel their ball is safe from defenders' hands when they hold it high above their head. This feature of the Australian high release allows shooters to give the target their total concentration.

To execute the shot, begin by facing the goalpost with your feet shoulder-width apart, body upright, and weight evenly balanced between both feet (see figure 4.1). Focus your eyes on the front middle rim of the goal ring. Rest the ball on the fingers of your shooting hand. Raise your shooting hand directly above your head until your arm is almost at full stretch. Make sure the centre of your elbow and wrist are in line with the goalpost. Place your non-shooting hand near or on the ball to steady it in readiness for the release.

Drop the wrist of your shooting hand backwards a few inches behind your head. As you drop the ball backwards, gently bend your knees. Using your fin-

---

FIGURE 4.1 | **KEYS TO SUCCESS**

AUSTRALIAN HIGH RELEASE

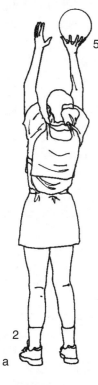

a
b

Preparation

1. Face the goalpost ___
2. Feet shoulder-width apart ___
3. Body balanced ___
4. Eyes focused on the front of the rim ___
5. Ball resting on the fingers (not the palm) ___
6. Wrist under ball ___
7. Wrist and elbow centred to goalpost ___
8. Knees bent ___

Execution

1. Drop wrist backwards a few inches behind the head ___
2. Flick ball with fingers and wrist ___
3. Aim to place ball high over rim ___
4. Guide release with index finger ___
5. Impart slight backspin with index finger ___
6. Extend knees slightly ___

Follow-Through

1. Point index finger to ground ___
2. Follow with fingers and wrist ___
3. Bring arms down ___

gers and wrist, flick the ball in a high arc to the goalpost, while at the same time extending your knees. Your index finger is the last to release the ball. It pulls down, imparting a backspin on the ball, and follows through to almost touch your palm. As your wrist follows through, by pointing to the ground, the ball travels in a high arc before dropping through the centre of the ring.

For shots taken in close proximity to the goalpost, very little leg movement is required. As the length of the shot increases, to generate more power to the shot you'll need to bend your knees as you drop the ball backwards. For shots near the edge of the goal circle, you can also use a small jump to gain extra distance.

How to Execute the Caribbean Shot

Begin by facing the goalpost. Place the foot on your shooting side just in front of the body, about half a stride. Put your other foot just behind your body. Your body is upright and well balanced, with your weight on your back foot, knees slightly bent (see figure 4.2). Focus your eyes on the centre of the rim of the goal ring. Rest the ball on the fingers of your shooting hand. Bend the elbow of this arm so the ball rests near your head. Position the centre of your elbow and wrist in line with the goalpost.

Climb your wrist and fingers straight up to release just before full extension. Release with a flick from your wrist and fingers. Guide the ball and impart a backspin with your index finger. The ball travels in a high arc over the rim of the goal ring. The backspin enables the ball to drop through the centre of the ring. Follow through with a downwards movement of your fingers and wrist. Transfer your weight onto the front foot to complete the follow-through.

For shots taken close to the goalpost, use very little leg movement. As you move away from the

goalpost, use your legs to generate more power on the shot. For very long shots, begin the movement with a strong upward push generated from your back leg.

Stepping Before a Shot

Shooters who use the Australian high release technique frequently apply the Footwork Rule to their advantage when a defender exerts strong pressure on the shot. A small sideways step often gives you the room you need to release the defender's pressure on the ball. Shooters also use the step to move closer to the goalpost when an appropriate opportunity arises, for example, when taking a penalty shot. You need to have sound basic shooting technique before you begin to step.

How to Execute the Step Before a Shot

As you take the catch, line up your shot and focus on the goalpost ready to release the ball (see figure 4.3) . Step quickly onto the non-grounded foot, which takes you away from the defender or closer to the goalpost. Transfer your weight onto this foot, which is initially flat. Now transfer the weight up onto the ball of your foot and release. Stay well balanced. Remember, if you re-ground your landed foot you will be penalised for stepping.

It requires a fairly experienced shooter to apply the step successfully. You need to know which foot you have landed on and be aware of the direction you need to step to gain an advantage for yourself. This is one of the game's advanced skills because you are shooting while balancing on one foot. Challenge yourself to attempt it when you are shooting successfully in match play.

FIGURE
4.2

KEYS TO SUCCESS

CARIBBEAN SHOT

a

b

c

Preparation

1. Focus on centre rim of the goal ring ___
2. Body balanced ___
3. Shooting foot forward ___
4. Weight on back foot ___
5. Ball on fingertips ___
6. Elbow bent ___
7. Ball at head height ___
8. Elbow and wrist centred to goalpost ___
9. Hand under ball ___

Execution

1. Climb arm until straight ___
2. Release just before full extension ___
3. Flick ball with wrist and fingers ___
4. Guide ball with index finger ___
5. Impart backspin with index finger ___
6. Ball travels in high arc to ring ___

Follow-Through

1. Point fingers and wrist down ___
2. Bring arm down ___
3. Transfer weight to front foot ___

FIGURE
4.3 **KEYS TO SUCCESS**

STEP BEFORE A SHOT

Preparation

1. Line up ball ___
2. Focus on front of ring ___
3. Body balanced ___
4. Elbow and wrist centred to goalpost ___

Execution

1. Step away from defender ___
2. Transfer weight ___
3. Hold grounded foot in air ___
4. Balance on ball of non-grounded foot ___
5. Remember the Footwork Rule ___
6. Release ball ___

Follow-Through

1. Bring grounded foot
   down ___
2. Move to post for
   rebound ___

SHOOTING SUCCESS STOPPERS

You will know as soon as the ball goes to the ring whether your shot at the goal is successful or not. Developing good technique helps you to achieve a high conversion rate. Here are some of the common errors that might hinder your technical development.

Error	Correction
Australian High Release	
1. The shot is flat.	1. Use three middle fingers on the release and impart backspin.
2. The shot falls short.	2. Extend your knees and legs before release.
3. You do not feel in control of the shot.	3. Spread fingers wider on the ball; shorten the drop of the wrist before release.
4. The shot skews right or left.	4. Follow through until all fingers point to the ground.
Caribbean Shot	
1. The shot hits the ring.	1. Raise your wrist and fingers straight up above your shoulder. Release the shot at the height of the climb.
2. The shot is too long.	2. Focus on the rim of the goal circle; reduce leg power.
3. The shot skews right or left.	3. Place your feet half a stride apart, shooting foot forward, facing the post. Keep body well balanced as you transfer your weight from the back to the front foot.
Step Before a Shot	
1. The defender is still able to pressure the release.	1. Lengthen your step. You are not gaining sufficient distance with the step.
2. You are off balance when you shoot.	2. Shorten the step; it is too long and you are overbalancing.
3. The shot is too long.	3. Take your step and then pause momentarily and focus on the goal ring before you release the shot.

SHOOTING

DRILLS

To become a very good shooter you need to practice daily. For beginners, a practice session should take about 10 minutes. Young athletes, up to 10 years of age, should work on a modified goalpost 8 feet (2.43 metres). As you begin to master the techniques, increase the session to 20 minutes. Older athletes should work for up to an hour, dividing the time into 15- or 20-minute sections.

The time spent on the components of a shooting session is determined by your yearly training program and the competitive fixture. Early in the season the emphasis is on technique, concentration and judgment. You might find that only one movement drill is included. At the business end of the season you might find that most of the session combines shooting with court movement and a defence of the shot. Technique and concentration drills are used more as a warm-up or for quiet sessions immediately before or after a major game.

1. Mirror Practice

Stand in front of a mirror and line your arms up to shoot. Practice the movement as you watch yourself in the mirror.

Success Goal = Shoot 5 imaginary goals using good form ____

Success Check
• The centre of your elbow points to the mirror ____
• The centre of your wrist points to the mirror ____
• Your arm is above the centre of your head ____
• You maintain elbow and wrist line when you drop your hand ____

2. Shooting With and Without the Goalpost

Stationary shooting allows you to concentrate on technique, line-up, release and follow-through.

a. Place the ball on your shooting hand. Drop your hand backwards a few inches and flick the ball a metre or two directly above your head.
b. Stand a step away from the goalpost, prepare to shoot, aim and release the ball so that it falls cleanly through the centre of the ring.

Success Goal =
a. The ball travels straight up from release 10 consecutive times ____
b. 3 successful goals ____

Success Check
• Body balanced ____
• Steady ball with non-shooting hand ____
• Focus on target ____
• Position arm and wrist in line ____
• Impart slight backspin on ball ____
• Ball arcs high on release ____
• Follow through with fingers and wrist ____

To Increase Difficulty
• Make the goals consecutive.
• Make the 3 consecutive goals fall cleanly without touching the ring.
• Increase your starting distance from the goalpost.
• Gradually increase the number of consecutive successful shots to 8.
• Place the ball on the ground at your shooting spot. Sprint forward 4 or 5 paces, turn, sprint back. Pick up the ball and shoot. Make 3 successful shots. Sprint between each one.

3. Shooting Cone Circuit

This drill enables you to concentrate on your technique and to make judgments on the distance of the shot. Place five cones at random in the front half of the goal circle. This means there is an imaginary line halfway between the goalpost and the top of the circle which dissects the circle in two. The cones are in the half that is closest to the goalpost. Begin by standing at the cone closest to the goalpost. When you have scored, move on to the next. Continue in this manner until you have scored at all five cones.

Success Goal = 1 goal scored from each cone ___

Success Check
- Focus on rim ___
- Judge distance to goalpost ___
- Keep body balanced ___
- Keep wrist and elbow centred to goalpost ___

To Increase Difficulty
- Reverse the starting order. Start at cone farthest from goalpost.
- Score 5 goals from 10 attempts.
- Score 5 goals consecutively.
- Reset the cones to a more challenging position.

4. Shuffle and Shoot

Working the shuffle and sidestep allows you to develop concentration and refine your judgement under pressure.

a. Start in close to the goalpost. Begin with a successful shot. Shuffle step backwards half your shoe length. From that position make another successful shot. Shuffle back as before. Move only when your shot is successful.

b. Stand about two metres from the goalpost. Begin with a successful shot. Take a small step sideways. From that position, make another successful shot. Take a small sidestep as before.

Using the success goals and variations stated previously, develop your ability to use the sidestep to go around the circle as well as you use the shuffle step to go forward and backward.

Success Goal =
a. 6 successful shots from 6 short backward shuffle steps ___
b. 6 successful shots from 6 sidesteps ___

Success Check
- Body balanced, ball steady ___
- Increase leg power in the shot slightly as you move away from goalpost ___
- Follow through with fingers and legs ___

To Increase Difficulty
- Score the goals from 10 attempts.
- Increase the steps to 8, then 10. Remember: you do not shuffle or sidestep until the goal is scored.
- Now try for 6 consecutive goals from 6 consecutive steps. Can you increase this to 8?
- Reverse the steps. Start at the edge of the goal circle and take a step forward when you score. Use the original success goal: 6 successful shots.
- Score 2 goals from each point before you take a step.
- Increase the length of your stepping gradually as your concentration and accuracy improve. The world's best shooters can start at the goalpost and step to the circle's edge before working in the reverse.
- Use a full step rather than a sidestep.

5. Move and Shoot

Once you are feeling confident in your shooting technique, begin to introduce a movement before you set for your shot. This brings the practice closer to match play. As a shooter you have to earn the ball before you can try to score a goal. Not only should you begin to move before you receive the ball to shoot, you should also start to follow the shot to the goalpost to contest a rebound. Here is a drill to practice this.

Place five cones at varying distances on the ground inside the goal circle. Place one marker five metres outside the circle. Your partner has the ball and is a metre away from the outside marker. Sprint to the outside marker, elevate to take a high ball from your partner. Return the pass and drive to the circle to take a long pass at the first marker. Balance yourself, steady the ball, focus on the goalpost and shoot. Follow your shot and rebound if unsuccessful. Once you have scored at the first marker, move to the next marker and start the drill again.

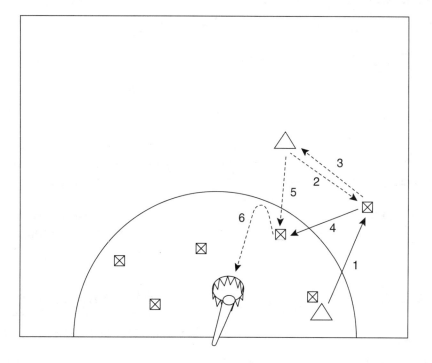

Success Goal = 1 goal scored from each marker ___

Success Check
- Accelerate quickly ___
- Watch the ball ___
- Balance before shooting ___
- Follow through to the goalpost for rebound after shot ___

To Increase Difficulty
- Score 5 goals from 8 attempts.
- Score three goals consecutively.
- Place two more markers further outside the circle. Use these to increase the amount of work you do before shooting. For example, run to the first marker outside the circle and change direction, sprint to the second marker where you take a low ball, backward shuffle to the third marker where you take a high ball before sprinting to the circle for the final pass and shot.

To Decrease Difficulty
- Use 3 markers inside the circle.

BISHOP BURTON COLLEGE
LIBRARY

6. Over the Defence

Adding defence of the shot brings you even closer to match-like conditions. Drive into the goal circle to take a pass from a feeder. As you line up the shot, have a defender take up a position 0.9 metres (3 feet) from your landed foot. The defender offers a defence of the shot by reaching forward and pressuring your shooting arm. Release the shot. Both players follow through to contest the rebound.

Success Goal = 4 successful goals from 6 attempts with a defender pressuring the shot ___

Success Check
• Body balanced ___
• Eyes on ring ___
• Control release with fingers ___
• Follow through with fingers and wrist ___
• Be aware of defender's pressure ___

To Increase Difficulty
• Defender pressures the shooter's movement outside the circle as well as on the shot.

7. Two-on-Two

This drill allows you to practice some basic footwork skills in the goal circle, combined with passing under light pressure. The two goal shooters stand inside the goal circle, and two defenders stand next to them. The feeder is outside the circle with the ball. The feeder calls "go" and passes to one of the shooters. The shooters must make three safe passes to each other before taking a shot for goal. Defenders must use the recovery step to gain legal distance, then raise arms to pressure the shot.

Success Goal = 2 goals scored from 3 attempts ___

Success Check
• Create space with movement ___
• Watch the ball ___
• Know where other players are ___
• Balance before shooting ___
• Follow through for rebound ___

To Increase Difficulty
• Have one shooter work against two defenders.
• Defend the feeder outside the circle.

To Decrease Difficulty
• Use one defending player rather than two.
• Use two feeders outside the circle.

8. Stepping to Shoot

This drill gives you practice stepping before a shot. Stand with a defender in the middle of the goal circle with the ball on the ground. Pick up the ball and assume a shooting position. The defender jumps back to the legal distance and raises hands to pressure the shot. Takes a small sideways step away from the defender before releasing the shot. Both players follow in to contest the rebound.

Success Goal = 3 successful goals using a step before you shoot ____

Success Check
• Maintain body balance ____
• Eyes on the ring ____
• Judge distance ____
• Maintain technique ____

To Increase Difficulty
• Move to the back half of the circle to start the drill.
• Have a feeder start the drill with a pass into the circle that both players contest.

SHOOTING SUCCESS SUMMARY

Shooting is one of the game's most important skills: goals win games. We have looked at the two most successful shooting techniques in the netball world: the Australian high release and the Caribbean shot. To be a successful shooter you need to develop sound technique, then learn how to apply this when being pressured by defenders. Use your mirror to check your line and make sure you involve your coach or teacher in checking your line and technique according to the Keys to Success checklist in figures 4.1 through 4.3. Recording your shooting percentages from match play is easy to do and provides very good feedback. Our top players like to consistently record game averages above 80%. If you are new to the game, aim for 50% and then work upwards.

STEP
5 ATTACKING: MAKE YOUR MOVE

Whenever your team has possession of the ball, it is in attack. Each team member works hard to bring the ball down the court to the shooters so they can score. There are 14 players on the court, all in their designated playing areas, and each has three seconds to handle the ball. No wonder attacking play is fast and furious.

You need to be quick: think quick and move quick. That makes good netball. Attacking moves need an element of surprise to keep your opponents guessing, which calls for variety in your attacking play. You can achieve this in two ways: first by having a number of attacking moves that you can offer, and second by timing the use of these moves to increase their effectiveness. So attacking play has two important ingredients—the movement itself and the timing used to execute it. In this chapter we look at both.

First you are introduced to the game's basic moves. The work you have done with movement in Step 3 forms an important basis for attacking moves. If you have been working hard at running, jumping and changing direction, you should handle this step with ease. If you are having difficulty with these movements, then a review of Step 3 will help. Next, once you are moving confidently with your basic attacking moves, we introduce timing. We look at some ways you can develop your sense of timing moves so that they work for you on court.

The attacking moves covered in this chapter—the drive, the dodge, the fake, the hold, and the roll—are basic to the game. It is by no means an exhaustive list. Learn the basics and then combine and extend them to create your own moves. Individual flair is an important ingredient for winning attacking play.

Why Are Attacking Moves Important?

To win a netball game you must out score your opponent. You need to deliver the ball to your shooters frequently so they can keep the goals coming. Attacking moves are used to give your team the best chance of successfully bringing the ball down court to your shooters.

Good attacking moves make it easier to pass the ball successfully. When they are well executed, team members can read each other's moves. There is no hesitation in releasing the ball and players are confident. They move well and they move the ball well too. Attacking play like this makes it difficult for your opponents to counteract.

On the other hand, attacking moves that are uncertain and hesitant cause the error rate to rise. Mistakes are more frequent when attacking moves are inconsistent and difficult for your team-mates to read. Attacking moves are important because they are the key to your team's attack. A team with good attacking moves provides many scoring opportunities, which is what successful netball is all about.

Attacking Movements

There is a lot to understand in attack. The drive, the dodge, the fake, the roll and the hold will get you moving on the court. To get up into the air you must jump. Just think of the havoc you can wreak on your opponent if you can combine these moves effectively! They will not know where you are or where you're going. When you see your opponent looking lost out there on court, you know that you have not only thought up a great move, but you have executed it to perfection.

Drive

As the name suggests, this is a powerful run to the ball. It can involve a few steps, or it can contain many. It can also include a change of direction. Starting from a balanced position with your weight down, assess the open court space you wish to move into and drive with your legs and arms, while preparing to take the pass. As you land and re-balance with a wide stance, look for your passing options (see figure 5.1). The important part of any drive is that you hit top speed in a few strides and that you maintain it throughout the movement. If you have worked at your take-off in Step 3, you have a powerful start to your drive.

Dodge

This is a simple change of direction. Use a low stance to transfer body weight quickly from one side to the other and back again. In the case of a double dodge, repeat the movement.

Fake

By offering a strong movement the upper body creates an illusion that the whole body is about to move in a certain direction. Dip your shoulder, arms and waist in the direction of the fake. However, keep your feet stationary. It is amazing how often you can fool your opponent into following a well-executed fake.

Hold

In netball the term hold is really synonymous with a screen in basketball, where you use your body to block out a player. Again, use a wide base. Your legs protect a space for you to move into, for a team member to use, or to block an opponent from moving into a space (see figure 5.2). The most common use of the hold is to protect space for taking a high ball in the circle and for taking the centre pass in the mid-court.

Roll

Use the roll to start an attacking move or counter a hold. It is a half-turn executed from a low, wide base. Your legs provide the wide base to execute the roll. Drop your weight down. Transfer your weight through the leg on your turning side. Pivot around this leg. Transfer your weight evenly through both legs after performing the half-turn.

Jumping or Elevating

Jumping from one or two feet to take the ball or to tap it on to a team-mate: In a game of netball you use these moves many times. There are occasions when you use the move on its own, and others when it is more effective if you combine moves. Employ your creative talents to experiment with combinations of moves. Discover what works best for you. Challenge yourself to find new ways of attacking. Make sure that your moves contain that element of surprise. Keep your opponents guessing. That makes your attacking play exciting and very difficult to defend.

FIGURE 5.1

KEYS TO SUCCESS

THE DRIVE

Preparation

1. Body balanced ___
2. Weight down ___
3. Head up ___
4. Assess court space ___

Execution

1. Move into space ___
2. Drive with legs ___
3. Use your arms ___
4. Hit top speed quickly ___
5. Prepare to take pass ___

Follow-Through

1. Land and balance ___
2. Look for passing options ___

FIGURE
5.2

KEYS TO SUCCESS

THE HOLD

a

b

Preparation

1. Wide base ____
2. Body upright ____
3. Watch ball and opponent ____

Execution

1. Feel strong, protect space ____
2. Focus on ball ____
3. Move to take ball ____

c

Follow-Through

1. Land and balance ____
2. Look to pass or shoot ____

ATTACKING SKILLS SUCCESS STOPPERS

If you are constantly beaten to the ball by your opponent, you need to carefully examine your attacking skills. First, check your starting position to ensure you are generating a powerful take-off. Then look at the variety of moves that you offer. Is it too limited?

If the problem is not in these two, then it must be related to your on-court execution of the moves, and this involves your timing. Poor timing makes a good move ineffective. Here are some common problems to consider in your analysis.

Error	Correction
1. You are constantly beaten to the ball.	1. Increase the power of your movement; lower your weight to start.
2. Your opponent stays with you.	2. Combine movements; you need variety. Try using the hold to protect your space.
3. You do not hold your space.	3. Widen your base and keep your weight down.
4. You become disoriented when you roll.	4. Turn your head at the last moment as your body completes the turn.

Coming to Terms With Attacking

There are three important terms that are used in regard to attack play. It is helpful to understand them, particularly as we are about to look at some attacking drills.

Offer

When you make an offer in netball, you simply execute an attacking move. You offer yourself to catch the ball. Use your speed and strength to produce a move that your team-mates can easily read.

Re-offer

If your first move is unsuccessful, make another. Remember, the player with the ball must pass or shoot within three seconds, so in attack you should decide early when your first move is beaten and quickly offer another.

Preliminary Move

A move used before you offer the main attacking move. A fake and a dodge are often used as preliminary moves. A well-executed preliminary move sends your opponent in one direction while you make your offer in the other.

Successful attack play not only involves working to the ball, the off-ball movement counts as well. It is all part of winning attack play. When you begin to work seriously at developing attacking skills, you'll need to work with others in small groups or with your team members. You are getting ready for court play, and your practice sessions should reflect this.

ATTACKING

DRILLS

Practice the attacking moves on your own to start with, then develop combinations. As you begin to master the attacking moves, pay extra attention to when you make your offer. Timing is crucial to success when you are attacking. As you will find when you begin to play this game, a lot happens in a very small space and a short amount of time. As you watch good netballers play you will notice that they just seem to know when to go. It looks so easy because their timing is so precise. To be effective, attacking moves require good timing. When you are comfortable with the attacking moves, use the drills to introduce the timing element to your attacking practice.

1. Single Attack Moves

These are best practiced in small groups as part of the warm-up routines. Indicate the move to practice (for example the drive). Select a partner to start the drill. You and your partner are about five to six metres apart. Your partner offers the attacking move—in this case a strong driving move—and you pass the ball. Place the pass so that your partner is fully extended to take the catch. Continually pass the ball between you and your partner as you offer your attacking moves. Once you have achieved your success goal with one attacking move, change to another. Use a single dodge in your new move.

Success Goal = 6 well-executed moves that result in you and your partner taking 6 safe catches ____

Success Check
• Read movement easily ____
• Work at top pace ____
• Eyes on ball ____
• Focus on safe catch ____

To Increase Difficulty
• Introduce a creative challenge (for example, players cannot repeat an attacking move before they reach the success goal).
• Every second move a player makes must combine the attacking move being practiced with another move, for example, before you drive you must use a fake or a dodge.
• Have three players work the drill. You'll need good judgment to avoid working the same space as your partner.
• Place a defending player between the attackers and allow her or him to apply light defence pressure.

To Decrease Difficulty
• Have one player throwing and the other practicing attacking moves. When the success goal has been achieved players change roles.

2. Front and Back

Five players are standing in a line behind one another. You are the feeder. Stand four to five metres in front, facing the attackers. Indicate the move(s) to be practiced (for example, dodge and drive). The first attacker offers the move. You pass. The attacker catches and pivots. The back player on the line now offers her or his move. The front attacker passes to that player. She or he catches, and throws a long ball back to you (the feeder). The first attacker moves to the back of the line and the drill begins again. When you have passed to everyone, you join the line of attackers and another player becomes the feeder.

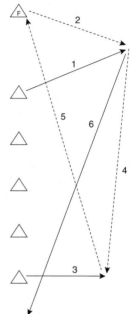

Success Goal = 1 successful front and back move and safe catch from each player in line ___

Success Check
• Confident moves ___
• Pass ball to outstretched hands ___

To Increase Difficulty
• Encourage players to be creative (for example, use a different move from the player you follow).
• Elevate to every third ball.
• Use a preliminary move before you offer.

3. Combining Attacking Moves

Four attacking players stand in line. You are the feeder. Stand about six metres in front of them with the ball. Indicate which attacking move to combine with others of the player's choice. For example, the instruction might be to combine moves with a dodge. While players are free to offer various combinations, the one rule is that players may not repeat a combination previously offered. The attacking moves should be powerful and easily read. As the feeder, you deliver the ball. The attacker returns the pass to you, who then passes to the next attacking player. Attackers go to the end of the line when they have successfully offered their moves and passed the ball.

When all four players have completed their attacking moves, change places with the first attacker. Restart the drill with a new attacking move to combine (for example, a two-foot elevation).

Success Goal = 1 successful combination of moves for each athlete in line ___

Success Check
• Quick attacking moves ___
• Body well balanced ___
• Watch the ball ___
• Read moves easily ___

To Increase Difficulty
• Have each athlete combine three attacking movements and take two passes from the feeder before moving to the back of the line.
• Place a floating defender between the feeder and attacker to pressure the movement and the pass.

4. Double Feed

Two feeders stand in front of a line of four players. They are about five metres from the players. Both feeders have a ball. To start the drill the first player offers an attacking move to the nearest feeder, who passes the ball accurately. The attacking player returns this ball to the feeder and then offers a different attacking move to the second feeder. The ball passes quickly between the feeders and attacker. As this attacker returns to the end of the line, the next attacker begins to make an offer to the first feeder. When the success goal has been reached, the feeders join the attacking line and two new feeders pass the ball.

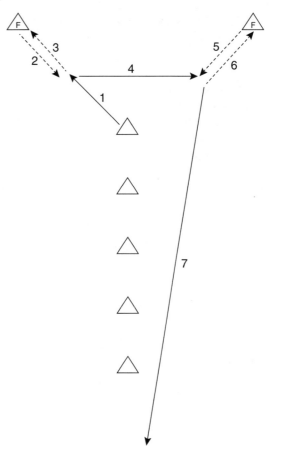

Success Goal = 2 successful moves from each player ___

Success Check
• Move strongly ___
• Read moves easily ___
• Flowing attacking movement ___

To Increase Difficulty
• The second attacker starts work when the first attacker returns the initial pass to the feeder. This means the attackers follow each other through the drill.
• Now increase your offers to three before the next player starts work. Make sure that all three moves are quite different. You have to think and move quickly to master this drill.
• Place a defender between thrower and attacker to pressure the pass.

5. Timing From the Throw

Work in pairs. You are the feeder so you have the ball. Stand five metres in front of your partner, the attacker. Both you and your partner face the same direction. Now, throw the ball to yourself by tossing it overhead and taking it head height directly in front. As you take the catch, turn to face attacker. The attacker watches the ball and reacts to the cue (the catch). The attacker offers a move. You release the ball. The attacker takes the catch safely, then returns the pass to you so you can begin the drill again.

Success Goal = 3 accurately timed attacking moves and successful catches ____

Success Check
- Weight down, ready to offer ____
- Body well balanced ____
- Watch the ball ____
- Offer strongly on cue ____

To Increase Difficulty
- As the feeder you begin to vary the height of the ball that you throw to start the drill.
- Vary the distance between yourself and the attacker for each pass.
- Change the cue and include a preliminary move: the attacker now times from the release of the ball that you play to yourself. The attacker uses a fake or roll as a preliminary movement when you let the ball go. If this is well timed, the attacker offers strongly when you catch and turn as before.
- Use the same cues as above, but work the drill in reverse order: drive to the ball initially, then drive away and elevate to take a high ball from the second cue (the catch).

To Decrease Difficulty
- Feeder calls "go" to indicate to the attacker when the move should start.

6. Work in Threes

You are the feeder. Stand five to six metres in front of your two attackers. The attackers are a similar distance apart. All players face the same way. Throw the ball overhead to yourself, catch and pivot. Attackers' cue is your catch and turn. Both attackers offer. You choose one attacking move and pass to that player. The other attacker re-offers on that catch and turns to receive the second pass. The second attacker passes the ball back to you to begin the drill again. When the success goal has been achieved, one of the attackers changes places with you.

Success Goal = 4 successful, well-timed moves and catches from each attacker ____

Success Check

• Read the cue ____
• Move at top speed ____
• Be aware of the other players' offers ____

To Increase Difficulty

• Introduce a new cue—the release of the feeder's overhead pass. Both players offer a fake or roll as a preliminary move on this cue. Then they drive on the original cue—your catch.
• Use the same cues but change the moves (for example, as the feeder plays the ball overhead, drive). On the original cue—your catch—one player drives, the other uses a hold and then elevates.
• Use the second pass as another cue. Have the free attacker and the feeder re-offer so a third pass can be made.

To Decrease Difficulty

• Have the feeder call to each attacker for the offer.

7. Work in a Line: Fours

Four players stand in a line about five metres apart. All players face the same direction. The timing cue is the catch. The first player throws the ball in the air, catches and turns, and the second player offers a move. The first player quickly releases a pass to the attacking second player, whose catch is the cue to trigger the next attacking move from the third player in the line.

Continue this pattern up and down the line of players with the players using any moves they choose.

Success Goal = 2 well-timed moves and catches for each player in line ___

Success Check
- Watch the ball ___
- Time the move from cue ___
- Use a variety of moves ___
- Attack strongly ___
- Move ball with speed ___

To Increase Difficulty
- Vary distance between players.
- Use a high ball on every second pass.
- Use a preliminary move on the first cue and a drive on the second cue (for example, the first cue is the player's move, you offer a dodge; the second cue is the player's catch and turn, you re-offer with a drive).
- Increase your line to 8 or 10 players who are evenly spaced the length of the court, all facing the same way. See if you can pass the ball up and down the line with all players executing well-timed moves.
- Ignore the first offer from each player and wait for them to re-offer before passing.
- Make every third pass a bounce pass or a high ball.
- Change the timing cue. Offer a preliminary move when the player in front of you begins her or his move.

To Decrease Difficulty
- Divide the large team into 2 lines of 4 or 5 players.

8. Give and Go

The team pairs off. Half go to one end of the court and half to the other. They are 12 metres apart facing each other in lines. Coach stands in the middle with the ball. Announce the timing cue (for example, the catch). The drill starts with the pair who are facing the coach both driving forward to offer.

The coach passes to one of the players. The first player catches the ball, giving the cue for the other player to re-offer. The partner produces a second attacking move and receives the ball. When both players have handled the ball, this is the cue for the pair at the opposite end to make their moves. Both players drive forward to offer. The ball is passed to either player. When the catch is taken, this is the cue for the partner to re-offer. When the ball is passed to this player it provides the cue for the third pair to drive forward and offer. As each pair concludes its moves the players continue through the working area to join the end of the opposite line.

Success Goal = 8 successful passes from well-timed moves without a drop ____

Success Check
• Watch the ball ____
• Read the cue ____
• Attack into open space ____
• Move ball accurately ____

To Increase Difficulty
• Have each pair make 3 successful passes before the next pair starts its moves.
• Place a floating defender in the middle of the working area to pressure the moves and pass.

To Decrease Difficulty
• Bring pairs in closer, about 6 metres. Reduce the handling so that each pair passes once before the next pair offer their attacking move.

ATTACKING SUCCESS SUMMARY

Attacking play requires a sound knowledge of the basic moves: the drive, hold, fake, roll and dodge serve you well on the ground, while you need to elevate to work the high ball. Once you have mastered these moves, combine them to create new ones. A well-timed attacking move is very difficult to defend. Train yourself to read the cues and you will execute your moves precisely. Before you move to the next step, ask a partner or instructor to use the checklist in figures 5.1 and 5.2 to evaluate your success on executing the drive and the hold.

STEP
6 DEFENDING: MAKE YOUR MARK

D efending in netball is a challenge. The fast flowing, high-scoring nature of the game means that the attacking skills receive a lot of attention. Moving the ball forward to the shooters in anticipation of a goal often appears more exciting than working the defence to deny your opponents possession.

Don't be fooled! Winning teams make sure they have a balance between defence and attack. Winning teams love to deny their opposition the ball, to force them into errors, to pressure them into making mistakes. The goal scored from a brilliant intercept brings the crowd to its feet. This is spectacular stuff: the plays people talk about long after the whistles have stopped and the game has ended.

Nobody said defence was easy. To make your mark you need persistence, along with some highly developed skills. And just for good measure there are a few important rules that specifically relate to defending.

Netball rules state that you may not contact a player from the other team in a way that interferes with that player's actions. When the umpire calls contact against you, a Penalty Pass is awarded to the opposition. If you contact in the goal circle, the shooter may take a Penalty Pass or a Penalty Pass or Shot. If you are penalised for contact, you will find yourself out of play, standing beside the thrower taking the penalty while the penalty is taken.

Obstruction is the other rule that you must understand to become an effective defender. To defend an opposing player with the ball, you must be 0.9 metres (3 feet) away from their landed foot to your nearer foot. This is why we need the recovery step, which we looked at in Step 3. The recovery step helps you to clear the distance between yourself and your opponent when you are beaten to the ball.

You obstruct when you defend within 0.9 metres (3 feet). If you obstruct, the umpire awards a Penalty Pass to the opposing team. If you obstruct in the goal circle, the shooter may take a Penalty Pass or a

Penalty Pass or Shot. In either case you must stand beside the thrower taking the penalty, out of play, while the penalty is taken.

Why Is Defending Important?

When you are defending you are trying to constantly pressure your opponent to cause them to make a mistake. Your team can then take possession of the ball and pass it down court for a shot at goal. Good defending allows your team to create more scoring opportunities by restricting your opponent's play. If the defending team is allowed to move or pass the ball when and where they choose, very few mistakes occur. This team then completely dictates the terms of play.

When you defend a team and begin to restrict its options, their error rate escalates. Good defending enables turnovers to occur. If you can capitalise on these opportunities, your team will be successful.

Each member of the team must be able to defend—defending is not simply about the three defence players being skilled. The most effective defence comes when the whole team applies pressure. Remember, the greater the pressure, the greater the reward. This simply means that a team's ability to defend successfully relates to all team members' willingness to pressure their opponent's moves and throws. Defending wins games. The difference between two teams is often not their ability to attack, but their ability to do the unglamorous work in defence.

How to Defend

There are a number of ways to defend. In this chapter we look at two key methods: one-on-one defence (shadowing) and defending off the player (anticipation). If you can master both of these techniques, you will have a very good foundation on which to build your defending skills.

One-on-One

The aim of defence is to dictate the terms of your opponent's attacking play and force a turnover of the ball. In one-on-one defence you aim to dictate the terms of attack before your opponent begins her or his move, and to maintain this situation throughout her or his move. This means that you will try to force your opponent to move where you want him or her to go, which of course will give you the best chance to intercept the pass.

For one-on-one defence, begin with a strong starting position: weight down, body well balanced, feet shoulder-width apart, hands held close to your body. You should begin on the ball side of your opponent, in front of your opponent, with your back turned to her or him, and have a view of her or him and the ball. This is known as the front stance (see figure 6.1a). Being on ball side means that the ball has to pass in front of you to reach your opponent. This gives you the best chance to intercept the pass.

Figure 6.1a The front stance places you in good position to intercept.

The starting position reflects the intent of your defence. The front stance is most commonly used when you wish to intercept. If you have to protect space, use the back start or a side stance. The back start, where you start immediately behind your attacker, acknowledges that you are prepared to sacrifice the front ball to protect the back space (see fig-ure 6.1b). Goal keepers often use this in their circle defence. They allow the long shot but protect the area close to the goalpost.

Figure 6.1b Protecting back space with the back stance.

Use the side stance to deny an attacker access to her or his strong move (see figure 6.1c). For example, if your opponent likes to lead to the right, you would begin your defence on that side and try to force her or him left.

Figure 6.1c Use the side stance to deny your opponent's strongest move.

No matter which stance you use, netball is a non-contact game. Your starting position should always be as close as you can get to make your presence felt without contacting.

Your starting position should give you the best chance for successful defending. This usually means that you should try to force your opponent wide, towards the side of the court. Carefully protect the busy central area of the court, the quickest route between both goals. If the attacking play flows quickly through here it is very difficult to stop. Forcing the ball wide slows the attack and gives you a greater chance of successful defending.

Watch the ball *and* your opponent. As your opponent moves, react and move in the same direction. As the ball is released, focus on it and extend fully to intercept. If you are unsuccessful at gaining possession of the ball, recover in front of your opponent and offer a defence of the pass, or defend any down-court move (see figure 6.2). Use the recovery step that we learnt in Step 3 to quickly clear the legal distance from the landed foot of your attacker. Raise your arms to pressure the pass, or crouch low to anticipate the throw. Both of these skills are discussed in this chapter. The more advanced skills of blocking your opponent's down-court move or dropping back to double-defend are covered in Step 8.

FIGURE 6.2

KEYS TO SUCCESS

DEFENDING ONE-ON-ONE

a

b

Preparation

1. Weight down ___
2. Body well balanced ___
3. Eyes on opponent and ball ___
4. Arms and hands close to your body ___
5. Feet shoulder-width apart ___
6. Protect central lane ___

Execution

1. Follow opponent's move ___
2. Maintain view of ball ___
3. Extend to intercept pass ___

c

Follow-Through

1. Use recovery step ___
2. Reposition in front of opponent ___
3. Pressure the pass ___

BISHOP BURTON COLLEGE
LIBRARY

Pressuring the Pass

Use the recovery step to reposition yourself in front of your opponent. Make sure you are the legal distance from your opponent's landed foot (0.9 metres/3 feet). Move your weight down so that you are well balanced. Extend both arms over the ball. Pressure the point of release of your opponent's pass—watch her or his throwing hand to anticipate the pass (see figure 6.3). Remember, you can reposition your hands, but not in an intimidating manner. For example, you cannot wave your hands around to try to put your opponent off. If your pressure is effective, your opponent focuses on you rather than on the team member who will be receiving the pass, and that is when mistakes are made.

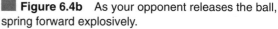

Figure 6.4a   Anticipating the pass with weight down and knees bent.

Figure 6.3   Pressuring the pass.

Anticipating the Pass

Recover in front of your opponent, keep your weight down and your body low, and watch the ball intently. As your opponent prepares to pass the ball, push your weight down strongly, and bend your knees so that you feel like a tightly coiled spring (see figure 6.4a). As your opponent releases the pass, spring forward at full stretch and try to intercept the ball (see figure 6.4b).

Defending off the Player

The aim of this defending play is to gain possession of the ball from the attacking team through an inter-

Figure 6.4b   As your opponent releases the ball, spring forward explosively.

ception. While you are aware of your opponent's movements, she or he is not pressured. The ball is the focus of your attention. You position yourself so you can drive hard to cut off an incoming pass. The element of surprise that such defence brings is a strength. It introduces an element of uncertainty to the attack, which can in turn increase the attacking team's error rate.

Watch the ball closely as it travels down court. Keep your weight low and body balanced. Judge the speed of the ball and the distance it is travelling. Remember that the long high ball gives you the best chance to cover ground. Decide which ball to intercept. Drive at top speed and take the ball at full extension (see figure 6.5).

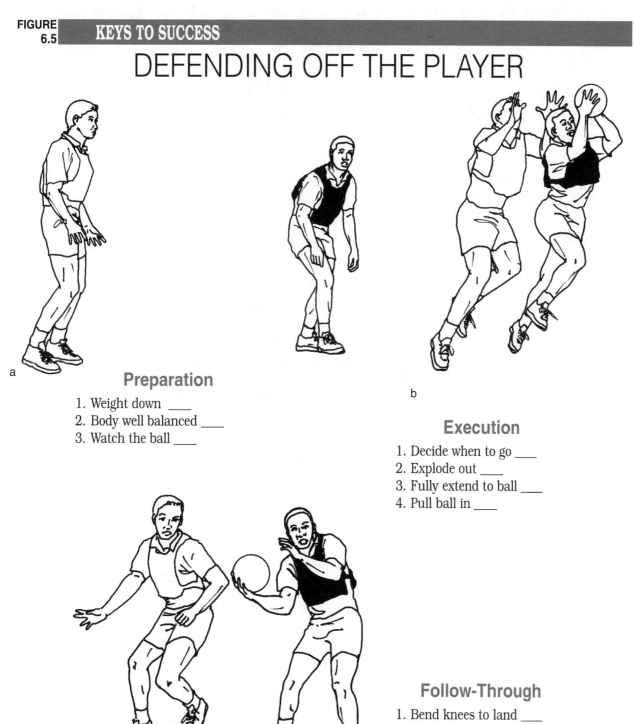

FIGURE 6.5

KEYS TO SUCCESS

DEFENDING OFF THE PLAYER

a

Preparation

1. Weight down ___
2. Body well balanced ___
3. Watch the ball ___

b

Execution

1. Decide when to go ___
2. Explode out ___
3. Fully extend to ball ___
4. Pull ball in ___

c

Follow-Through

1. Bend knees to land ___
2. Balance ___
3. Scan for attacking cue ___
4. Look to pass ___

DEFENCE SUCCESS STOPPERS

The most common errors in defence are contact and obstruction. Poor starting positions and lack of body control cause contacts. The umpire calls obstruction when the defender fails to clear the legal distance before defending a player with the ball. Defenders should be trained to automatically recognise this distance (0.9 metres/3 feet). Use a tape or stick to measure this distance during practice, paint a line on the ground to work beside, or use the diameter of the centre circle for recovery work.

Error	Correction
One-on-One Defence	
1. Attacker loses you in first few steps.	1. Adjust your starting position; you are too close to your opponent.
2. Attacker beats you in last few strides.	2. Focus on the ball when it is released.
3. You lose sight of the ball when you start to defend.	3. Keep your head up. Open your starting position by taking another step away from your opponent. This will give you a broader view of the court.
4. You are penalised for contact when you start to defend.	4. Adjust your starting position so there is more space between you and your opponent.
5. You are penalised for contact when the attacker takes the ball.	5. Make the decision to contest the ball sooner.
6. You are penalised for obstruction.	6. Use the recovery step to clear the distance. Land before raising your hands.
Defending off the Player	
1. You miss the ball.	1. Make the decision to contest the ball sooner.
2. You drop the ball.	2. Focus on the ball as you drive to intercept. Use proper catching technique.

DEFENCE

DRILLS

Defending requires you to make decisions with regard to your move, your opponent's move and the pass that is coming in. The drills need to focus on these aspects. You will notice that the drills are done in small groups; it is very difficult to practice defending by yourself.

1. Shadowing

You are the defender and your partner the attacker. Take a starting position for one-on-one defence. Call "go". When the attacker moves you must stay close for three seconds. Work hard to shadow every move.

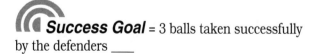**Success Goal** = 3 seconds of staying close to your partner with good one-on-one defence ____

Success Check
• Body well balanced ____
• Weight down ____
• Eyes on opponent and court ____
• Feet shoulder-width apart ____
• Arms close to body ____
• Move directly from the start ____

To Increase Difficulty
• Change your starting position to the opposite side, to the back and finally to the front. Have a player stand out in front of you with the ball. Now keep both your partner and the ball in view while you work.
• When you have achieved your success goal from these positions, have the player with the ball pass to your partner. Try to deflect or intercept the ball.

2. Line Defence

Three attackers and their defenders stand in a line facing the feeder, who has the ball. The defenders wear bibs to distinguish them from the attackers. The first attacker prepares to offer. You, as the first defender, take up a good starting position to force the attacker wide. The attacker offers and you react to the move. Try to intercept the pass from the feeder.

The successful player returns the ball to the feeder. As the ball is returning to the feeder, the next attacker and defender start the drill. After achieving the success goal, attackers and defenders change roles.

Success Goal = 3 balls taken successfully by the defenders ____

Success Check
• Position well at start ____
• Force attacker wide ____
• Watch ball and attacker ____
• React quickly ____

**To Increase Difficulty**
• Have each attacker try to take 2 consecutive passes. The defender must recover if beaten on the first ball and pressure the second move.

3. Pick Off

Two throwers stand about four metres apart and send shoulder passes between themselves. Four defenders stand in between them, but about five metres to one side. As the first defender, you watch the first pass, judging its flight. As the thrower releases the second pass, run at full speed to intercept. If you have watched the first ball well, you should be able to estimate where the best chance to intercept is. The next defender repeats the process.

Success Goal = 1 successful interception of the second pass for all four defenders ___

Success Check
- Judge flight of ball ___
- Keep weight down ___
- Estimate intercept ___
- Explode out ___
- Take ball at full stretch ___

To Increase Difficulty
- Intercept the first ball.
- Throwers vary passes. Use high balls and flat balls and include some bounce passes.
- Throwers and defenders vary the distance of their starting positions.

To Decrease Difficulty
- Coach calls "go" to help the defender to time her or his move.
- Defenders start the drill in closer to throwers.

4. Defending the Pass

The thrower has the ball. You stand next to your opponent about five metres away from the thrower. Your opponent offers to take a pass. The thrower releases the ball. You contest, but allow your opponent to take the pass. As soon as your opponent takes the catch, drop your weight and execute the recovery step that we learned in Step 3. Use both legs to jump back and clear the legal space. Now quickly raise your hands and pressure your opponent's throwing action. Reach out with both arms and hands, but be careful not to overbalance or you will obstruct.

Your opponent passes to the thrower, who drives behind your opponent to take the pass. You are successful if your opponent delivers a poor pass or is called for a held ball. When the thrower has possession of the ball, restart the drill.

Success Goal = 5 successful executions of defence pressure on the attacking pass ___

Success Check
- Recover quickly ___
- Clear legal distance ___
- Hold arms and hands up ___
- Apply pressure to throwing arm ___

To Increase Difficulty
- Have your opponent work an offer and re-offer before taking the pass. You must defend well enough to be able to contest the pass in, and then recover to pressure the pass out.

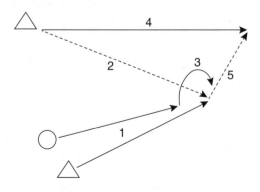

5. Pressure Work

Two throwers stand 10 metres apart facing each other; one has the ball. Two defenders and one attacker stand in the middle of the throwers. The attacker offers a move to start the drill. As one of the defenders, you react and try to cut off the pass. You or the other defender are successful if you intercept, tip or deflect the ball, or if the attacker drops the ball. The throwers and the attacker keep passing the ball between themselves.

 **Success Goal** = 3 successful interceptions by the defenders ____

 **To Increase Difficulty**
• Add another attacker to the middle area.

✔ **Success Check**
• Watch the ball and the attacker ____
• Keep weight down ____
• Move strongly ____
• Decide when you can intercept ____
• Go hard to the ball ____
• Recover if beaten ____
• Defend again ____

6. Square Defence

Mark an eight-metre square with four cones. Four throwers stand one on each side of the square; one has the ball. Two defenders and an attacker are inside the square. To start the drill the throwers and attacker work together to keep the ball moving. The only rule is that they cannot pass the ball back to the player they received the ball from.

The defenders have to work every ball: drive hard, try for the intercept, recover and pressure the ball if unsuccessful. When they reach the success goal, together with the attacker they change places with the throwers and start the drill again.

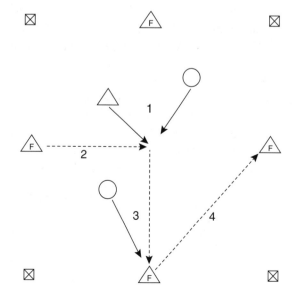

Success Goal = 3 successful defence touches or intercepts ____

✔ **Success Check**
• Anticipate the pass ____
• Move quickly to intercept ____
• Recover if beaten ____
• Defend again ____

To Increase Difficulty
• Work until you have 5 successful defence touches.
• Move the markers out 2 metres. Have another attacker and defender in the square.
• Add another attacker in the square.

7. Defender in the Middle

In the following drills, you are not shadowing your partner and chasing her or him across the court. You are learning to sit back and focus on both the ball and player movements, waiting for your chance to intercept the right pass. If you can learn to anticipate well on court, you will cause many problems for your opponents.

a. Three throwers form a triangle five or six metres apart. You are the defender in the middle of the triangle. The throwers pass the ball around between themselves, varying the type of pass they use. You watch the ball and decide when to intercept. Run hard to take the ball, then return the ball to a thrower to start the drill again. When your reach the success goal, change places with a thrower and restart the drill.

b. Two throwers stand facing each other three metres apart; one has the ball. You are the defender and stand behind the thrower without the ball. The throwers use a two-handed straight pass to each other and attempt to keep the ball moving between themselves. You use a figure 8 movement to move between and around the throwers, trying to intercept each pass. When you have attempted to intercept eight passes, change places with one of the throwers and start the drill again.

 **Success Goal** =

a. 2 touches or intercepts ___
b. 4 balls out of 8 passes successfully taken by defender ___

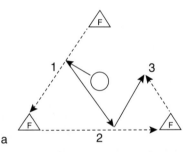

a

✔ **Success Check**

• Keep weight down ___
• Decide when to intercept ___
• Drive strongly ___
• Extend to ball ___
• Move around feeders without contact ___

To Increase Difficulty

• In drill *a*, increase your success goal to 4.
• The throwers are allowed to move. Mark off an appropriate working space with cones. Throwers can move within this area as they pass to one another.
• In drill *b*, take 6 balls from 10 attempts.
• Vary the passes to include high and low balls.
• Defenders begin in the reverse position so they are not facing the ball as they start the drill or when they pass behind the feeder.
• Increase the distance between throwers by another metre.

To Decrease Difficulty

• Use a very slow pass between the feeders until the defender gains confidence.

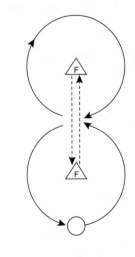

b

DEFENDING SUCCESS SUMMARY

Defending has important rules that you need to understand to be successful. Review your checklist in figures 6.2 and 6.5 as you practice. Although at times it might appear to lack the excitement and attention that attacking play has, sound defence wins games. If you are prepared to work at defending, success will come. There is nothing more exhilarating than being able to take a brilliant intercept. It unsettles the opposition while sending your team's confidence sky high. Work at denying your opposition as many opportunities as you can. Don't be afraid to run out and take that screamer. It will make your day!

STEP 7

COMBINING SKILLS: PUTTING IT ALL TOGETHER

So far we have looked at all of the game's basic skills: catching, throwing, body movements, footwork, attacking and defending. In preparation for match play it is now time to put these basics together—to combine skills. In this step we use a number of ways to achieve this: drills, minor games, and modified games.

The drills we have used to date have been designed to practice the specific skill the chapter has presented. The drills in this step, however, are designed to get you to use two or three skills at once, or in very quick succession. In netball, when you go on court to play a game you need to be able to do two or three things almost simultaneously.

Minor and modified games are not played alone or even in small groups; they are usually kept for team practice times.

Minor games are great for practicing the individual skills we have previously learnt. The competitiveness of the game situation allows you to build patterns of play that become the basis of team play. Minor games also provide an opportunity for the coach and the athletes to develop their sense of teamwork: to support and encourage each other's efforts and to advise in a constructive manner. In addition, they are fun.

Modified games combine skills. Modifying the rules of netball brings us close to match conditions. There are a number of ways to do this, for example, modify the court to use only one third, change the positional play so that players rotate when a goal is scored, or eliminate the defence of a shot at goal. Each allows you to gain confidence on the court before you take part in competitive match play.

Don't forget that the skills and practices we have introduced so far do not represent a finite list. In this fast-moving game you need to think quickly and look for new ways of doing things. Be creative—the new and the original add another dimension to your play.

Why Is Combining Skills Important?

On the netball court, skills are not used in isolation. When you handle the ball you have to catch, land, pivot, read the attacking and the timing cue, and then pass the ball—all within three seconds. That is busy! Also, your opponent will probably be defending you all this time.

Combining skills enables you to practice in match-like conditions. It challenges you to do two or three things simultaneously or in sequence. It also helps you to understand the significance of the skills we have learned so far.

How to Combine Drills

You have already gained some experience of joining movements together—remember in Step 5 where you had to offer and then re-offer your attacking moves? The success of these moves depends on your ability to read the play and react to the opportunities that you can create. Timing your moves is crucial: arriving too soon or too late can nullify all your hard work, so watch for the cues and time your work precisely.

Double-Play

Successful execution of the double-play leaves you feeling good. It also helps move the ball very rapidly in attack. The centre and wing attack frequently use double-play at the centre pass, while defenders use it to bring the ball out of the back third.

A double-play requires good judgment of court space and well-timed moves. As the name suggests, a player initiates two attacking plays in quick succession, passing the ball to a team-mate in between. To execute a double-play, the attacker takes possession of the ball from a centre pass or throw in. She or he makes a quick pass off to a team-mate nearby, and then offers a strong down-court drive to take the next pass.

FIGURE
7.1

KEYS TO SUCCESS

THE DOUBLE-PLAY

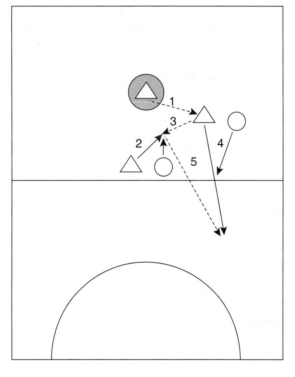

Preparation
1. Take possession of ball (1) ___
2. Scan down court ___
3. Keep body balanced ___
4. Move weight down ___

Execution
1. Pass off (3) ___
2. Drive down court (4) ___
3. Keep eyes on ball ___
4. Extend to take pass (5) ___

Follow-Through
1. Land and balance ___
2. Look for passing options ___

COMBINING SKILLS

DRILLS

In netball terms, when we talk of combining skills we refer to combining the basic skills of attack and defence into short bursts of play. The explosive nature of this game requires players to switch from one role to the other and back again in a very short space of time. The drills and games in this step enable you to begin to experience these on-court demands.

1. Passing Under Pressure

You have worked at throwing techniques and developing an accurate pass. Now it is time to put your knowledge and skills to the test by placing them under some strong defending. To be successful in this drill you need to work on the third aspect of passing: selecting the right pass. You are now working the throw in the same way as you do on court.

Mark the right half of a third with cones. Have three attackers and one defender stand in this area. Nominate each attacker to be either first, second, or third. The attackers move freely in this court space passing the ball between themselves. Each time the first attacker catches the ball the defender quickly puts a strong defence on her or his pass. When this attacker has achieved the success goal, replace the defender with a new player who pressures the second attacker's pass. Rotate players so each gets a chance at being both an attacker and a defender.

Success Goal = 3 successful passes from each attacking player whose pass is being pressured ___

Success Check
- Attackers assess the defence ___
- Select and execute pass accurately ___
- Defence focuses on attackers and the ball ___

To Increase Difficulty
- Add a second defender who applies some defence to either of the two attackers who are not under defence pressure on their pass.
- Add a third defender. Each attacker is now under full defence pressure on their move and pass.
- Finally, add a fourth defender to allow a double defence on an attacking player's pass. Each time a player releases the ball, two defenders have their arms outstretched pressuring the pass. This amount of pressure tests the attacker's ability to accurately select and execute the appropriate pass.

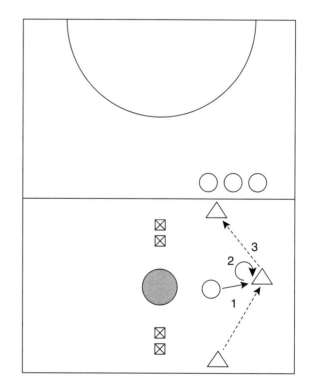

2. Across the Third

You can work this drill across any third of the court. It begins with a simple form involving three players: two attackers and one defender. By increasing the difficulty, it develops into a challenging drill with three attackers and four defenders. To start play, two attackers stand on the sideline outside the court area; one has the ball. The defender is on the court. The attacker without the ball enters the playing area. The other attacker passes the ball to the on-court attacker as he or she travels across the third. The defender applies pressure to either player as they move across the third.

The attackers keep passing to each other and try to reach the other side of the court without losing possession of the ball. The defender tries to force an error. When both attackers achieve their success goal, rotate the players' positions to take the ball back across the third. When the defender achieves her or his goal by causing an attacking error, substitute another defender so the first defender can have a rest. The attackers return to their starting positions and restart their run across the third.

Success Goal = Keep possession of the ball until attacking players have reached the far sideline across the third ____

Success Check
- Attackers offer strongly ____
- Read the move ____
- Select pass and execute precisely ____
- Defenders focus on player and the ball ____
- Judge the pass ____
- Explode to ball ____
- Recover and persist ____

To Increase Difficulty
- Add another attacker and defender so the numbers are now three attackers playing and two defenders.
- Even-up the ratio by adding a third defender; it is now three attackers on three defenders.
- Overload the defenders by adding another player to their side; this makes it three attackers and four defenders. The additional defender really tests your attacking skills.

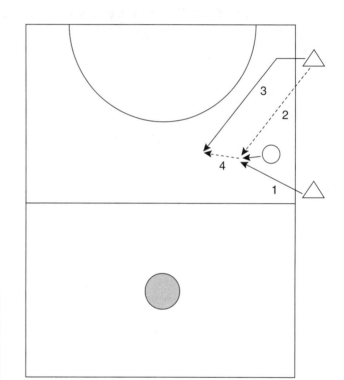

3. Square Ball

Four players are on each team: team A and team B. Each team wears a different coloured bib. Use cones to mark a 12-metre square on the playing court. Three members of each team stand inside the square. The fourth member is the substitute player and stands outside the square. The attacking team must work within the square.

Start the drill with team A in possession of the ball and team B in defence. Team A passes the ball between themselves until they make an error. The coach umpires the rules of play within the square and calls an error when the attacking team loses possession of the ball, or when a member of the attacking team commits a rule violation.

Team B takes possession of the ball when an error occurs and attempts to beat team A's score. As each team concludes its attacking attempt by making an error, the substitute player enters the square and rotates a position within the team. Both teams have three attempts at scoring the highest number of passes while in attack.

Success Goal = To score the most successful attacking passes from 3 attempts with possession ___

Success Check
• Maintain defence pressure ___
• Attack and execute confidently ___
• Change roles quickly and smoothly ___

To Increase Difficulty
• Vary the size of the square.
• Overload the defending play. Allow the substitute player to enter the square as an extra player when the team is in defence. This means that there are three attacking players inside the square and their substitute outside, while on the defending team all players are in the square.

To Decrease Difficulty
• Remove a defender from the play.

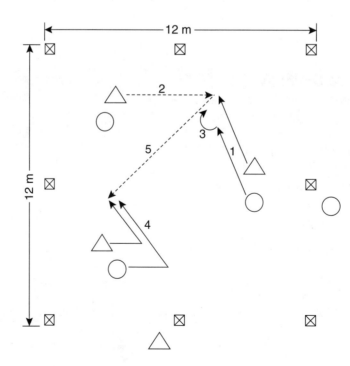

4. Down-Court Attack

Divide the court in half long ways, from goal line to goal line. Organise two teams of six players; both teams wear coloured bibs. Team A is in attack and its members are in two groups of three behind the goal line. Team B is in defence with two members on court in each third. Team A tries to bring the ball down court. The three players work together to keep possession of the ball as they take it from one goal line down the court to the other. As the attackers enter each third the two defenders of team B try to force an error. If they achieve this, the attackers run down court ends. When both groups from team A have attempted their down-court attack, change the teams' roles.

Success Goal = First team to score 3 successful down-court attacks with all players handling the ball ___

Success Check
• View long court ___
• Work spaces in attack ___
• Maintain pressure in defence ___

To Increase Difficulty
• Reduce the attacking group to two players. This means the attacking team lines up in pairs. All three pairs attempt to bring the ball down court before the teams change over.

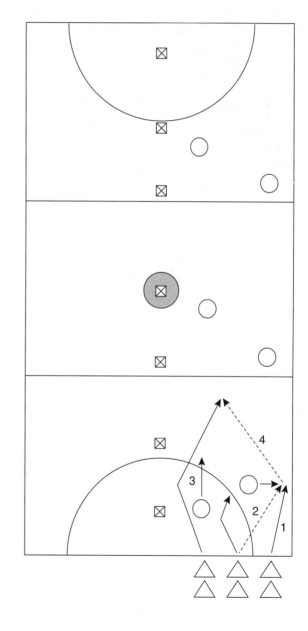

5. Two in Each Third

This drill is similar to Drill 4, but more court-related. The attacking team is on court in the same way as the defenders: two in each third. The attackers start with the ball at one end and must bring it safely down court. All players are restricted to the third of the court in which they start. Each player on the attacking team must handle the ball. The coach or umpire blows the whistle to start play. Each time the attacking team reaches the success goal, it scores one point. The ball remains with the attackers until they make an error. When the attacking team makes an error, take the ball to the opposite end of the court and change the teams' roles. Restart play. The winning team is the one that first scores three points.

Success Goal = First team to score 3 successful down-court attacks with all players handling the ball ___

Success Check

• View long court ___
• Work spaces in attack ___
• Maintain pressure in defence ___

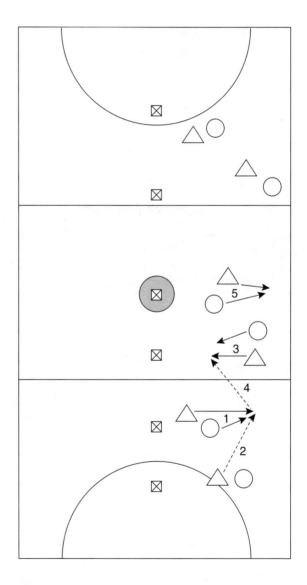

6. Minor Game: End Ball

In this game the ball travels up and down the court. You attack and defend the ball as you do in a game of netball. Use either the full length of the court, or one of the end thirds. Organise two teams of equal numbers, and designate one player from each team as the end player. If you are using the full court, the end player stands in the goal circle; if you are using one third of the court, she or he stands in a hoop beyond the sideline. Space out the rest of the team evenly, each with an opponent in a one-on-one style. Start the game at the centre of the area with a toss-up between different pairs each time.

When a team passes the ball successfully down court to its end player, it scores one point. It scores an extra point if this is converted into a goal (if you are using goalposts). The team must make at least three throws before the end player can catch the ball. If a player drops the ball, the game starts by the opposing team throwing into play from the end player's area. After a scoring, change the end player and start the drill again with another pair taking the toss-up in the centre.

If you are playing with very young players, allow them six seconds to handle the ball. Also allow them to shuffle their feet. Older players should use the netball rules of three-seconds possession, no contact or obstruction, and adhere to the Footwork Rule.

Success Goal = First team to score 5 goals wins ____

Success Check
• Attackers find open space ____
• Control the ball ____
• Body well balanced ____
• Read attack moves easily ____
• Apply defence pressure ____

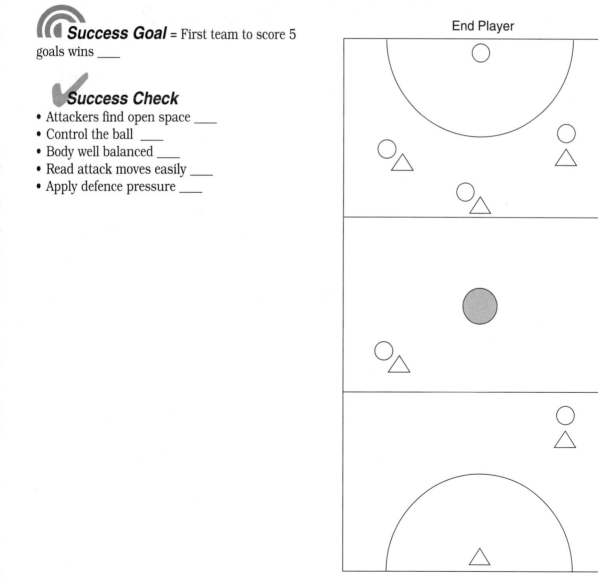

End Player

End Player

7. Minor Game: Island Ball

In this game the defenders have to back their judgement to intercept, while the attackers require accurate, quick passing. Use cones to mark an area 8 metres by 16 metres, and divide this area into two side-by-side courts. Organise two teams of six players. Four members of team A stand in the corners of their court, and four members of team B stand in the corners of their court. These players are the "Islanders". The remaining two players are the defenders and they stand in the middle of their opponent's court.

Start the game with a toss up between a pair of defenders on the centre line. The winner passes the ball to her or his team's court. The Islanders pass the ball between themselves while the defenders try to intercept and pass the ball across to their side. A team scores a point when its Islanders pass four consecutive passes. When a point is scored, change one defender with an Islander.

Success Goal = First team to score 10 points wins ___

Success Check
• Watch the ball ___
• Pass accurately ___
• Decide which ball to intercept ___
• Drive hard and extend toward the ball ___

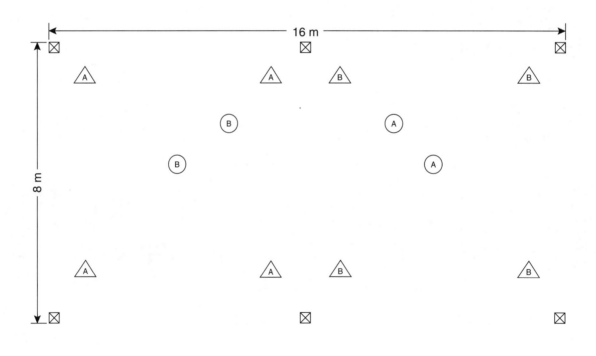

8. Minor Game: Numbers

This game helps you to improve your passing in attack and your anticipation skills in defence. Mark off the centre half of one third of the court with cones. Number each attacker as 1, 2, 3 or 4. Play a game of "keeping off" between the four attackers with the ball and two defenders wearing coloured bibs. The attackers must call a number as they throw. Six successful passes score one point for the attackers. The defenders score by touching the ball or by forcing the catching attackers outside the marked area. When a team reaches the success goal, two defenders and attackers change places.

Success Goal = First side to score 5 points wins ___

Success Check
- Accurate passes ___
- Strong moves in attack ___
- Pressure defence to cause error ___

9. Modified Game: One Third

This game uses two teams of five players. Use one third of the netball court with two portable goalposts in the middle of each sideline. In each team designate two attackers, two defenders and a centre, and position them as shown in the figure.

Rules

- Teams toss for ends and centre pass. The winning captain elects to take the pass or identify the team's goal end.
- Only the two attacking players in your team can shoot for goal.
- One point is scored if a shot hits the goal ring and two points if it passes through.
- Play restarts with a centre pass after each score. Centre players take turns to pass the ball.
- Players rotate positions after each score.
- You are allowed six seconds to pass and you may take two steps with the ball. (As players become more adept, apply the normal rules of the game.)

Success Goal = First team to score 10 points wins ___

Success Check
- Move into open space ___
- Choose correct pass ___
- Keep body well balanced ___
- Apply pressure in defence ___

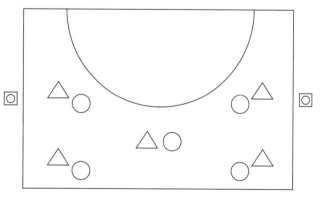

10. Modified Game: Half-Court

The game is played in one half of the netball court. Each team has seven players: four are on court, the remainder are the interchange players. Each team has two players in the goal third, one player in the centre third, and one player in the centre circle. One umpire controls the game.

Rules

- Teams toss for possession of opening centre pass.
- Only the two attacking players in the goal third can score a goal.
- Players must have the ball inside the goal circle before the shooter can shoot for goal. Each goal scores one point.
- After a goal is scored, restart play with a centre pass. Teams alternate the centre pass and their attacking and defending roles. Players rotate positions after each goal.
- If a defending player intercepts the ball, the defending team must pass the ball back to their centre in the centre third. When the defending centre takes possession of the ball, the teams change roles.
- Players may have six seconds to pass the ball. They also may take two steps or shuffle on the spot. (As players become more adept, apply the normal rules of the game.)

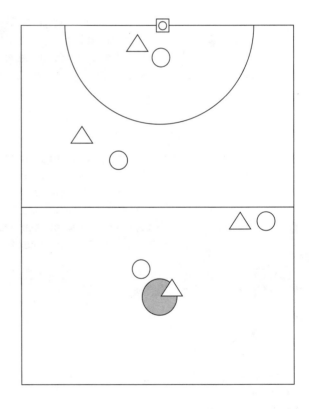

Success Goal = First team to score 5 goals wins ___

Success Check
- Strong attacking play ___
- Persistent defence ___
- Adjust to umpire's calls ___

11. Modified Game: Full-Court

Two teams of seven players position ready to play. Restrict players to the areas of play as defined by the rules of netball.

Rules

- Teams toss for the centre pass. The winning captain elects to take the pass or identify the team's goal end.
- The centre pass alternates throughout the game.
- Each goal scores one point.
- The ball must be touched in each third of the court.
- Players must pass within six seconds.
- Players may shuffle on the spot when landing.
- The shot at goal cannot be defended.
- A ball passing out of court is thrown in by the team that did not touch it last.
- Play 5-minute quarters, rotating positions at the end of each quarter.

Success Goal = The team with the highest score at the end of four quarters of play wins ____

Success Check
- Change from attack to defence quickly ____
- Adjust to umpire's calls ____
- Encourage team-mates ____

COMBINING SKILLS SUCCESS SUMMARY

You have now worked at putting movements together in preparation for match play. When combining skills, begin your practice with simple routines. After you have completed the drills, ask a trained observer or instructor to check your fundamentals, using the Keys to Success illustrated in figure 7.1. As you accomplish your success goal, move on to more vigorous challenges. The games and drills in this step not only test your on-court skills, they help you to understand the importance of working with others. Being part of a team is what this game is all about.

STEP

8

TEAM PLAY: STRATEGIES AND SPACE

Being a member of a netball team provides many challenges. The best team members are those who make a positive contribution to the total team effort. Make sure you work at this. You will not maximise your talents unless you learn to work with others. Assess the strengths and weaknesses of yourself and your team-mates. Play to your strengths in competition, and work to improve your weaknesses in training.

Remember that the effective combination of the skills of seven athletes makes a much more formidable team than the efforts of a few individual stars. That does not imply that great teams do not have their stars—they do—but that is not all they have. The team members working with those really talented athletes also have important roles and functions to fulfil. They do not sit back and let the stars do all the work. Make sure your team acknowledges each player's importance. When everyone feels part of the team, you are on your way to being successful.

Why Are Team Play Skills Important?

The netball court can become quite congested. Fourteen athletes working on a relatively small court space have the potential to cause chaos. Team skills allow you to organise the court space effectively, which lays a strong foundation for the team's success.

Early netball team strategies tended to adopt a very rigid approach where set plays, called "systems", were practiced relentlessly. The modern approach is to have one or two basic strategies for attacking and defending from which the team builds its playing patterns. Being creative and encouraging individual flair is important to successful teams.

Make sure you spend as much time on developing space awareness as you do developing strate-

gies. Do not rigorously drill system play; it encourages athletes to simply follow instructions instead of fostering creativity and adaptability to specific challenges. Team skills should challenge athletes to think on court. Thinking players make winning teams. Some simple strategies for attacking and defending will assist you to organise your team effectively.

Three-Option Attack Strategy

One of the basic strategies upon which teams build patterns revolves around a three-option attack. Whenever your team has possession, the player with the ball should have three passing options.

1. The first option is to pass to a player who leads strongly and is in front of her or his opponent. This lead, which should be offered quickly, is easily read and is initiated as soon as the catch is taken. Experienced teams can even initiate the offer before the catch is taken.
2. The second option is to pass to an alternate front move. This player makes a judgement on the likely success of the first offer, and moves when it becomes clear that the first offer has been too well defended and the player with the ball is in trouble.
3. The third option is a backup that is usually generated from behind the player with the ball. It is the safety valve, and is offered quickly and surely. Sometimes this is just a simple back pass to allow the attack to re-offer. At other times the player uses a long high ball to move the ball away from the congested area of play.

Often the second and third moves are not made, or if offered, are not needed or not used. They should, however, be ready to come. In a really close game, the team who has all three options operating puts itself in a strong position for success.

Applying the Strategy

We will now look at common scenarios and show basic strategies for moving the ball down court. These examples are not hard and fast rules; they are simply ways that you can apply the three-option strategy. The first, second and third options are represented by the numbers in the figure below. Be creative and interpret the plan around the plays that work for your team. It might be that your team can deliver the long ball accurately, so your strategy should acknowledge this. Once the ball has passed the half-way line, the first attacking move should be offered in the circle. In this instance, "look in" to the goal circle is the basis of your strategy. Rather than making a more conventional short pass, the team focuses on the goal circle and looks to send the long ball in to the shooter as the first move, even from the centre circle.

In the Back Third

Rebound Taken by Goal Keeper

Wing defence offers the first down-court move. Centre offers the second down-court move. The goal defence provides the backup.

Sideline Throw In From Goal Defence

Wing defence offers the first down-court move. Centre provides the alternative option and the goal keeper is the backup.

Baseline Throw In From Goal Keeper

Goal defence offers first, wing defence follows and centre provides the backup. In this case, with play starting on the goal line, the backup is provided by the centre who drives into the back third to move a long ball through. This simply means she or he takes a long ball just inside the transverse line which allows the ball to travel quickly over the third. Obviously the move cannot be generated from behind the player with the ball.

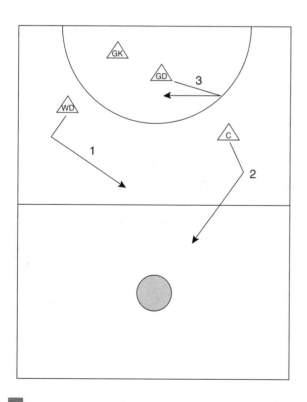

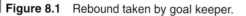
Figure 8.1   Rebound taken by goal keeper.

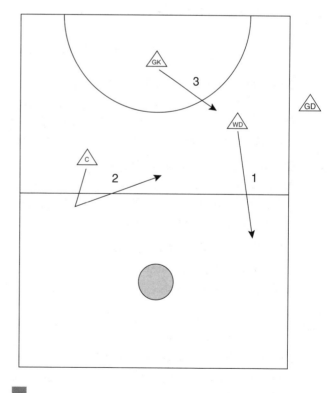

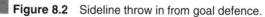
Figure 8.2   Sideline throw in from goal defence.

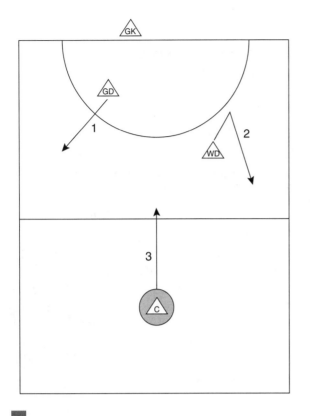

Figure 8.3 Baseline throw in from goal keeper.

In the Centre Third

Sideline Throw In From Wing Defence

Use this when the wing defence has the ball close to the transverse line. Centre provides the first offer, wing attack the second and goal defence is the safety valve.

Centre With Ball in Back Third

Wing defence drives hard down court to move the ball through mid-court. Wing attack is the second option and goal defence is the safety valve.

Wing Defence With Ball in Centre Third

Centre offers first, wing attack offers second and goal defence provides the safety valve.

In the Front Third

Centre With Ball Mid-Court

The attack uses the shooter on the lead. Goal shooter offers first, wing attack provides the alternative and wing defence is the backup.

Goal Shooter With Ball Near Transverse Line

Shooter looks in the goal circle first. Goal attack offers first, wing attack second and wing defence is the backup.

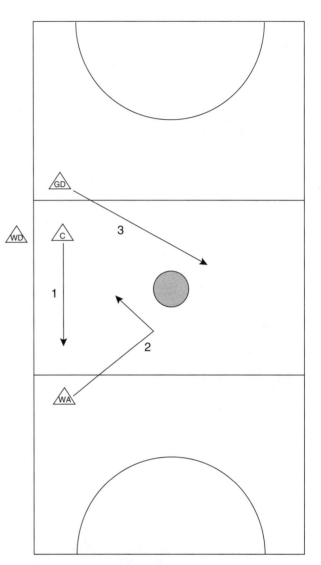

Figure 8.4 Sideline throw in from wing defence.

Goal Attack With Ball Outside the Goal Circle

Goal attack looks into the goal circle first. Goal shooter offers first, wing attack is ready with a second offer and the centre provides the backup.

Young players might find it difficult to have three moves organised for each throw. When players are learning the game there is so much to think about: getting their feet under control, passing the ball accurately, timing the offer, and reading the move. The best approach to applying strategies is to break down each strategy into its basic formula and then build it over time to the situations that are outlined in the previous descriptions.

To do this, concentrate on the first move. Each time your team has possession, only one player takes

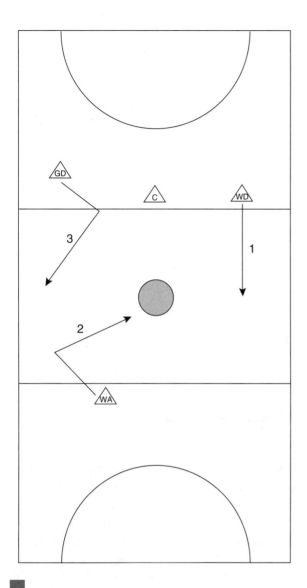

Figure 8.5   Centre with ball in back third.

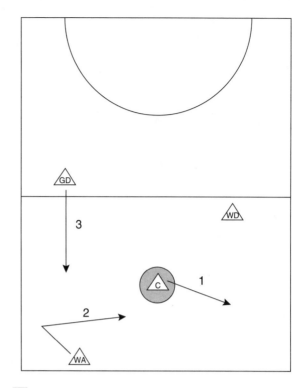

Figure 8.6   Wing defence with ball in centre third.

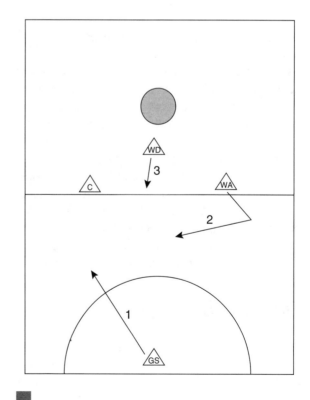

Figure 8.7   Centre with ball mid-court.

responsibility for making a successful attacking move. The thrower waits only for this attacker, waiting for a successful break to come. The attacker keeps offering and re-offering for the full three seconds. This approach allows time for the attacker to try two or three variations of the move. The weakness with this one-player approach is that there are no alternatives for passing.

Team practice time should be used to develop an understanding of, and confidence in, team strategy. As a player, tell your coach how the strategy feels on court. Then begin to apply the strategy in match play, making sure you support each other. Acknowledge plays that work well.

When your team is using the first lead well, introduce a second option. Use the backup (safety valve)

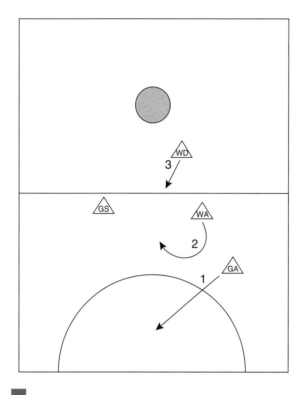

Figure 8.8 Goal shooter with ball near transverse line.

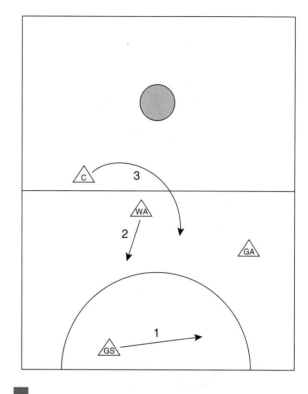

Figure 8.9 Goal attack with ball outside the goal circle.

option before you use the second forward offer. It is important to not to be locked into thinking that the ball must always travel forward. Introducing the backup move as the second part of the strategy reinforces the fact that keeping possession is more important than passing forward. Successful teams understand this principle well.

You might find, as a young athlete, that your team is working well with just the two options available. Then don't force the issue. Polish what you do and keep it simple and working rather than complex and confusing. Finally, introduce the third part of the strategy when the team needs a new challenge. At this time use the second forward offer.

Defence Strategy

Pressure, pressure, pressure and then a little surprise. After reading Step 6, you know that defending is the non-glamorous part of court work. The rules often seem biased against the defending player. To be successful, the defence strategy must work with all seven players trying to restrict their opponents' opportunities. Leaving defending to the back-line

defenders is a recipe for disaster. The best defence strategy involves a commitment from all team members to apply defensive pressure.

Focus on the defensive pattern that works best for your team. I have always favoured one-on-one as the basic strategy. It enables team members to take responsibility for their own player. While zone defence and the press (both discussed later in this step) develop good anticipation skills and can certainly cause teams to become unsettled, they do not exert the strong pressure over the total time of play that one-on-one achieves. If you pressure well all match, you are likely to be rewarded for your efforts in the final minutes of each quarter and the last passages of the match. After setting the basic strategies, look for plays that add variety and assist team members who simply cannot contain their opponent.

The key to success in defence is the amount of pressure you generate. Many players work diligently to cover the first move and when they are unsuccessful simply drift out of play. To develop an effective defence strategy, team members must work before the ball comes in and continue to work long after the initial attacking lead. When you have unsuccessfully defended your opponent's initial move, regroup your efforts and apply pressure again. Teams that have the ability to do this can exert the type of pressure that wins matches.

Let's look at some ways of applying pressure.

Double-Defence

Every time the ball goes out of court and has to be thrown in, the defending team has a player advantage on court. Use it well. The most common way to do this is to place a double-defence on the player likely to receive the first pass on court. You can also use the double-defence to nullify dominant players on the opposition team, particularly the wing attack at the centre pass or an outstanding goal shooter. In Step 10 we look at the double-defence at the centre pass, and in Step 11 in the goal circle.

The key to successful use of a double-defence is to position early and wisely. Both players need to be positioned before the attacker begins her or his move. Stand close, about a step away, from the attacker. Offset so that one takes the front side, and the other has the back. The front player should be ball side. Now work those legs and keep the pressure on as the attacker begins to move.

You can also apply double-defence as an alternative to pressuring the pass when your initial efforts to defend have been unsuccessful. As your opponent takes the pass, quickly size up just where you think the ball will be thrown. Drop back into that passing lane and try to provide additional pressure on the attacking lead coming out to meet the ball. In this situation, you are watching the ball, with little view of the attacker behind you. Your team-mates should talk to you to guide and encourage you. Work with your team-mates to position yourself effectively. Listen for their calls and respond. If the attacker suddenly finds she or he has two defenders to contend with, you might cause her or him to react and a mistake may well follow.

Although a double-defence seems easy to apply, it is not. You and the other defender position yourselves so that both of you restrict the most beneficial options for the attacker. Work together to maintain this close pressure and if the pass is made, both of you contest the catch. It is surprising how often you see the double-defence work the initial move quite strongly and then have only one of the pair contest the pass. Reducing the pressure in this way means you do not maximise the benefit of the double-defence. If the attacker receives the pass, one defender should use the recovery step and pressure the pass. The other should pick up the undefended player.

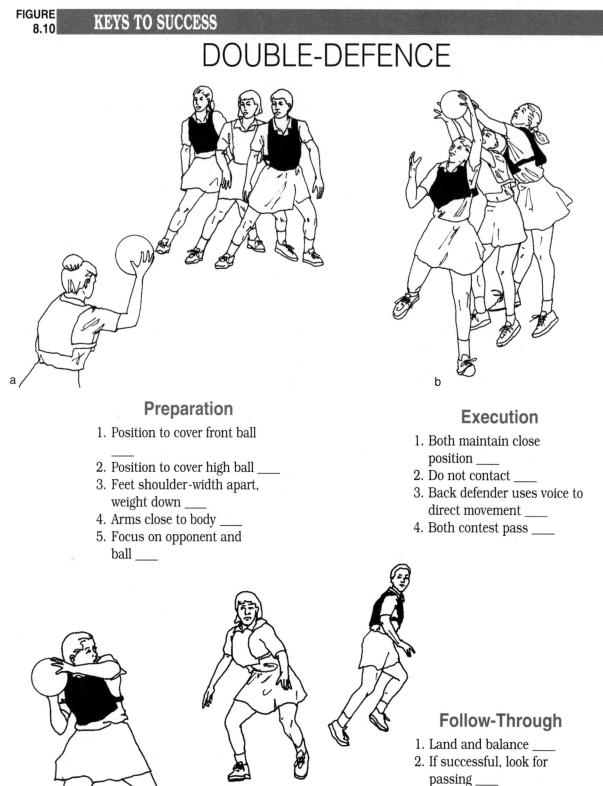

FIGURE 8.10

KEYS TO SUCCESS

DOUBLE-DEFENCE

Preparation

1. Position to cover front ball ___
2. Position to cover high ball ___
3. Feet shoulder-width apart, weight down ___
4. Arms close to body ___
5. Focus on opponent and ball ___

Execution

1. Both maintain close position ___
2. Do not contact ___
3. Back defender uses voice to direct movement ___
4. Both contest pass ___

Follow-Through

1. Land and balance ___
2. If successful, look for passing ___
3. If unsuccessful, split ___
4. One recover and pressure pass ___
5. One pick up player re-entering court ___

Defending the Down-Court Space

This is another way that you can offer further defence when your initial defence move is unsuccessful. Use the recovery step and position yourself directly in the line of attack in which your opponent wants to move. Wait for your opponent to pass; keep your weight down, a wide base and a strong upright position. As soon as your opponent releases the ball, begin to defend so that you block off the down-court route. Work hard to hold up the attacker by using rapid sidesteps from side to side to stay in front of her or him. Make the attacker go very wide around you. As you are facing the attacker you are concentrating primarily on her or his movements. Although you should be aware of the ball, you do not focus on it. Holding up your opponent is of major importance. Remember, the rules do not allow you to cause a contact with the attacker. Have the attacker cause it—that is good defending.

Figure 8.11 Use rapid sidesteps to block off down-court moves.

Press

The press is a term used to describe a type of defence that targets a specific court area where there is a high chance of applying pressure to secure a turnover. The defence players press the area, overloading it and trying to force an error. Use this very useful strategy intermittently to break up attacking play that is flowing too freely. Here are two ways to apply this strategy.

Press at the Transverse Line

This can be used when the ball is coming out of the back third near the transverse line. Use this strategy after a throw in as it allows time for players to set up. Three players of the defending team quickly leave their opponents and form a triangle at the top of the centre third, near the transverse line of the attacking team's goal end. Their aim is to protect the centre corridor. The goal attack and wing attack are about a metre behind the transverse line and the centre is another metre or so behind them, towards the centre circle. All players have their weight low and use rapid sidesteps across the area to cut off space.

The attacking team is often thrown by this tactic and releases a wild pass. Another option attackers often use is to send a long, high ball down the side of the third. This should be easy for your wing defence or goal defence to intercept.

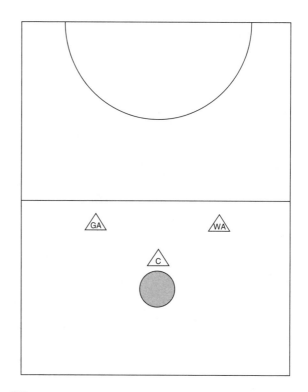

Figure 8.12 A three-player press protects the centre corridor.

Press Across the Centre Third

This can be used when the ball is coming down court to the opponent's goal end. All five players move quickly to the centre third when the call is given to set the press. Again, if it is set from a throw in, players have adequate time to prepare. The goal attack and wing attack set a little deeper in the centre third than in the preceding strategy. They are two or three metres behind the transverse line and the centre is about a metre in front of the centre circle. Players are mobile, working the ground surrounding them with rapid sidesteps. They move up to pressure the ball should it enter their immediate area and try to pressure the attack into sending up a high ball so that the back defenders can run and intercept.

Your defence strategy should have the one-on-one defence as its foundation. After making the initial move you should recover and exert more pressure on the pass and the player. Develop your repertoire to include defending off the player, double-defence, and the press, so you can introduce surprise elements that can unsettle the opposition. Remember to keep strategies alive and growing or they will become redundant and easy for the attacking team to beat. You can introduce periods of play where you come off the hard, chasing work and apply an anticipation-based approach to your defence. (Refer to "defending off the player" in Step 6.) Such tactics can help change the tempo of a game—a valuable ploy in tight encounters.

Space

Space is a precious commodity on the netball court—there is not a lot available. The game revolves around the ability to create space, to occupy it, and to defend it. Understanding the importance of space on the netball court helps you to become a thinking player. A player who is aware of the need to find open space and use it wisely can make a good contribution to team play.

Whether in attack or defence, you should think about space. In attack you are looking for ways to open the space so that you can take the pass. In defence you need to know where those openings are so that you can cut them off from your opponent. Your awareness of space should not be restricted to your own playing needs; you should also consider what space the players around you are using or will use.

Using space is really the final ingredient of good play. We have looked at the moves, understood the terms and worked at our timing. If you can do all this and use court space well, you will have much success on the netball court. The drills in the final part of this step are designed to develop your awareness of space.

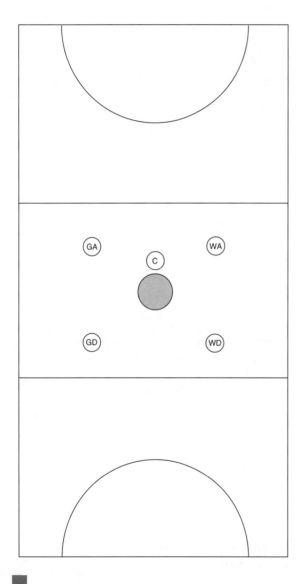

Figure 8.13 A five-player press across the centre third.

STRATEGIES AND SPACE

DRILLS

The following drills are designed to help you build team strategies in attack and defence, and build your on-court awareness of space. They are designed to allow players to move freely within the court to open space, and to teach players to use it well when working with other players. Of course, in defence we are trying to deny our opponent the use of this space. We are now very close to that all-important match play, so work hard on these final touches to give a very polished first performance.

1. The First Move

The three back line players—goal keeper, goal defence, and wing defence—are in the back third with the centre high in the centre third. Goal keeper has the ball on the goal line and is preparing to take a throw in. As soon as the goal keeper steps behind the goal line the coach calls "play". Players then offer the first move in their team plan to bring the ball across the back third into the centre third. Goal defence offers first, while the wing defence and centre are ready with alternate moves. When the goal defence takes the pass, the wing defence offers her or his first move; the goal keeper and centre are now ready to backup. The wing defence passes to the centre player in the centre third as the goal defence and wing defence backup. The ball has now travelled across the complete third.

Success Goal = All four players combine to successfully bring the ball across the third ___

Success Check
• Move strongly into open space ___
• Be aware of other players ___
• Pass accurately ___
• Acknowledge each other's good play ___

To Increase Difficulty
• Ignore a first lead from one player and use a backup. Did you lose momentum before you achieved your success goal?
• Have the wing defence and the goal defence change roles. This means that the goal keeper passes to the wing defence, who then looks for the goal defence.
• Start the drill on the court. Have both defenders near the goalpost for a rebound. Coach shoots and misses, the defenders rebound and play the ball to the wing defence, who plays on to the centre.
• Start the drill with the goal defence taking a side-line throw in. The ball goes to the wing defence and then on to the centre.
• Repeat the exercise but add some attackers to defend. Use two at first and allow them to float between players. Add a third and then a fourth as the attacking confidence of the team grows.
• Use the examples listed in the attacking strategy to work the mid-court and the front end.
• Finally, put all players on court and link the three sections' play so that the ball can travel the full length of the court.

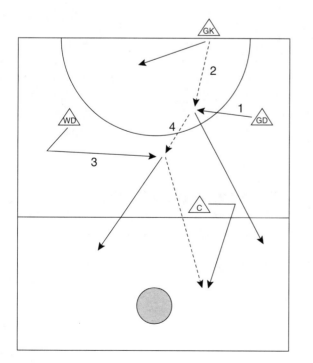

2. Facing-Up

Stand beside your opponent ready to defend. The thrower is about six metres in front of you and a receiver a similar distance behind you. Your opponent moves to take the first pass. You go with your partner, but you allow her or him to take the catch. Use the recovery step to clear the legal distance, keep your weight down and focus on your player. Your opponent passes off to the receiver and then drives down court to make a double-play. Let the pass go. As soon as your opponent begins to drive, work your feet quickly across the space so your partner has to work hard to pass you. Without contacting, you are trying to block the fast route down court.

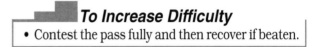

Success Goal = 2 successful defences of the down-court space that slows the attacker's drive ___

To Increase Difficulty
• Contest the pass fully and then recover if beaten.

Success Check
• Do not cause contact ___
• Knees bent ___
• Back upright ___
• Sidestep quickly ___
• Watch your opponent ___

3. Doubling-Up

Here are two drills to practice the double-defence. Remember to work together and to avoid contact.

a. Thrower is immediately behind the sideline ready to take a throw in. Attacker is on court, five or six metres in front of the thrower. Defenders apply a double-defence to the attacker. One defender positions between the attacker and the ball to cut off the front ball, and the other is on the opposite side, to the back of the attacker, to contain the high ball. Coach calls "play". The attacker offers and the defenders try to stay close to the attacker so that they can contest the pass.

b. The thrower stands on court with the ball, beside a defender. Another defender and attacker are three to four metres away. The thrower throws the ball into the air and jumps to take the catch. The defender jumps but does not contest the catch. They land and immediately the defender drops back to form a double-defence on the other attacker. The thrower attempts to pass successfully.

Success Goal = 3 successful double-defences where the defenders deny the attacker possession ___

To Increase Difficulty
• Add another attacker and defender who can offer to the first ball. The double-defence now has to split to pick up the original thrower when the new attacker has the ball.

Success Check
• Players work together ___
• Voice guides partner ___
• No contact ___
• Both defenders contest pass ___

4. Press

There are two parts to this drill. The press operates on a triangle formation which reacts to the position of the ball. Begin with the simple formation, a line press, and then practice the centre court press.

a. Three players are in a triangle formation in the centre third, near the transverse line. Two players are at the front and are about two metres from the line and six metres apart. The third player is about six metres away, in the middle behind them, near the centre circle. Two throwers are in front of the triangle, in the goal third, with the ball. As they move freely about in front of the press they pass the ball to each other. The triangle reacts to the position of the ball by moving up to pressure the pass when it comes to either side (diagrams a and b), or down the middle (diagram c).

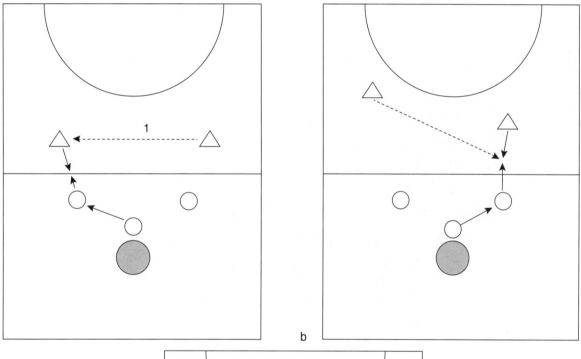

a   b

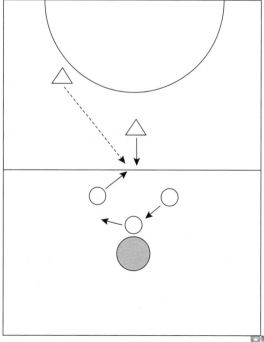

c

BISHOP BURTON COLLEGE
LIBRARY

b. Add two players behind the line press in the centre third to form the back triangle in the centre third (see diagrams a-c). Notice that the centre connects both groups. The back triangle reacts to the ball in the same way as the front players.

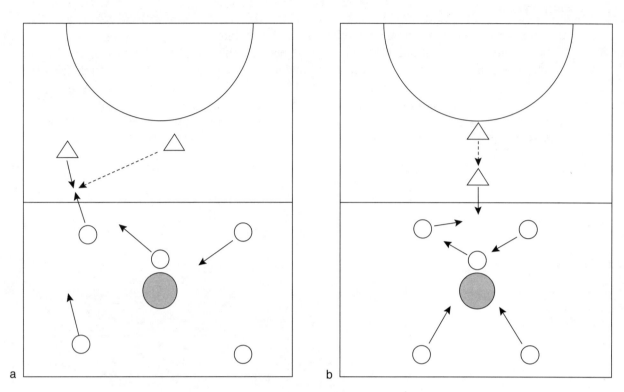

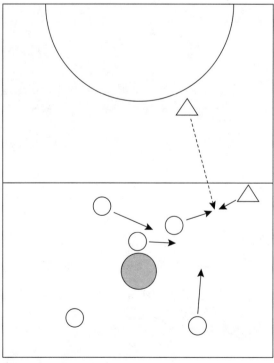

Success Goal = Press reacts successfully to six passes ____

Success Check

- Focus on ball ____
- Weight down ____
- React to ball ____
- Maintain triangle formation ____
- Explode to intercept the pass ____

To Increase Difficulty

- A receiver comes on court and works behind the defenders. The throwers now have the option to try to pass the ball to the receiver. When the ball is passed, the nearest player runs to intercept. The success goal is now to intercept three passes.
- Add a second receiver to the back of the defenders and try to achieve three intercepts.
- Add a third player who works in the middle of the triangle. Make sure that short balls cannot get through. Force the ball up in to the air and you will enjoy success.

5. Third Passing

Three attacking players are in one third of the court. One player throws and catches the ball to start play. The other two players offer simultaneously, using their court space well. The player with the ball selects the offer and passes the ball. The new thrower now has two leads offered, so she or he selects a player and passes. The three players move the ball between them as they work in their court space; the chosen third of the court. Each thrower has two players offering moves, and the moves should occupy different spaces. If both players lead to the same space, stop the drill, correct the players and restart the drill.

In any one practice session, do this drill in two or three segments. Start with the success goal, and when this has been reached, do the drill once with a condition. For the final segment use two defenders. At the next practice follow a similar format but change the condition you introduce. Over the course of the season increase the difficulty. Remember, players should achieve success before they increase their challenge.

Success Goal = 10 consecutive passes to athletes who use their space well ____

Success Check

- Look for space ____
- Read your team members' movements ____
- Use your voice to call the play when needed ____
- Offer strong moves that are easily read ____
- Watch the ball ____

To Increase Difficulty

- Every third pass must be a high ball.
- All leads are confined to five steps.
- There must be a bounce pass and a high ball in every five passes.
- Player X must hold the space and not lead; on every second ball you can pass only to a player who has made a re-offer.
- Introduce the defence. Begin with two. When the success goal has been reached add the third defender.
- If you really want to close the space add a fourth defender. In this case, reduce the success goal to six consecutive successful passes where players use space well.

6. Two-Thirds Passing

There are now three players in each of two adjoining thirds of the court. The drill starts in one third. Each player in one third handles the ball before passing into the adjoining third. Simply pass the ball back and forth from third to third. All three players offer and handle the ball before passing it across the transverse line. Again you should be looking to see that all players offer into space.

Success Goal = 12 consecutive passes to players who use space well ___

Success Check
• Maintain momentum ___
• Open space ___
• Pass precisely ___
• Be aware of other players ___

To Increase Difficulty
• The first player to handle the ball as it enters the third must re-handle it before passing it back into the other third.
• Take only two passes before passing the ball back into the other third.
• You must use a long throw to pass across the transverse line.
• You can only use a two-handed pass to deliver the ball.
• One player must use a preliminary move every time the ball enters your third.
• Now add the defence as suggested in the previous drill.

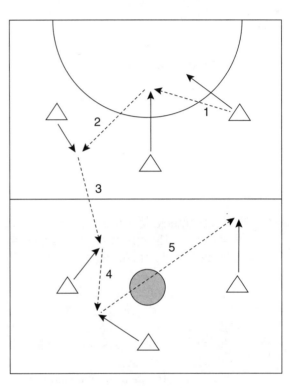

7. Full-Court Passing

There are now three players in each third of the court. The ball starts at one end and travels up and down the court without a handling error or players using the same space.

The limit to this drill is really your imagination. After attempting the conditions below, create your own. Relate them to the performance of your team; then add defence. This really challenges your ability to find space. Try to incorporate two or three short bursts of this work in each team session. You will notice that your ability to find space and use it wisely really starts to develop.

Success Goal = The ball travels up court and returns, with all players using space well and no handling errors ___

✔ Success Check

- Look for space ___
- Move to space ___
- Watch movement and ball ___
- Read timing cues ___
- Offer strongly ___
- Pass accurately ___

To Increase Difficulty

- One player in each third must use a preliminary move.
- After the ball crosses the transverse line into the new third, pass it back to the third it came from before passing it forward to the next third.
- All players must offer simultaneously when the ball crosses the transverse line but only one is used.
- You must use a high ball to cross the transverse line.
- All players must use one hand to catch and throw.
- Only use high balls.
- Add defence.

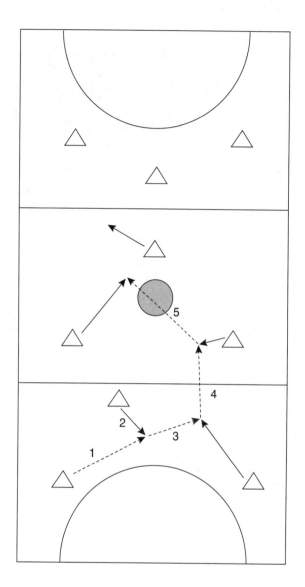

TEAM PLAY SUCCESS SUMMARY

We have now looked at the final parts of our preparation for match play. You are now ready to take to the court and see how well you can put it all together. If you have worked hard you should find you are able to cope quite well with that all-important first game. Now that you are playing, make sure you keep learning and developing your skills. Ask your coach to evaluate your technique, using both the checklist in figure 8.10 as well as those provided in Steps 1 through 7. The final steps, specialising by thirds, provide some very specific and challenging work to help you become a very good player.

STEP 9

THE BACK THIRD: FOCUS ON DEFENCE

The division of the netball court into thirds provides a unique characteristic of the game—each third requires players to develop certain skills and tactics so they can play effectively within that court space. These last three steps look at each third and focus on the skills that will assist you to perform well in your chosen area of the court.

The back third is home for your defensive specialists, who aim to restrict the opposition from scoring. The centre third is for the athletic players who love to run. They link the defence and attack thirds, have the most court space to cover and need to run all game. The front third is where the attacking specialists work; they produce the team's score.

When you first play netball, make sure you have a run in each third. You can then choose your preferred third from experience. Consider your strengths and the composition of your team before you nominate your position.

The two key players in the back third are the goal keeper and the goal defence. The main objective of these players is to restrict the opposition's shooting opportunities. The wing defence and the centre also play within the back third, but their court space is restricted to the outside of the goal circle. They cannot defend within the circle—the last line of defence.

When the ball enters the goal circle, the centre and the wing defence players should constantly reposition themselves on the circle's edge so that they can provide support for their defenders. This might involve retrieving loose balls that have been deflected or tapped to them, or defending their opponent so that shooters cannot pass the ball out to their team-mates. Once a defender gains possession, the wing defence and the centre should offer strong attacking moves to drive the ball down court towards their own goal.

Why Is Specialising in the Back Third Important?

As the team's last line of defence, your defending skills need to be more fully developed than your team-mates'. When your goalers allow the ball through their area, other players such as the centre can try to stop it further down court. When the back line players let a pass into the goal circle, your opponents can score. If your back line can exert enough pressure throughout the match, then they can wear the opposition down. When your opponents have to work hard for every ball in their attacking end, they drop balls and miss goals. On the other hand, the shooting percentages rise when the ball flows into the goal circle easily.

Defenders need to develop a good understanding both with each other and with their outside players, the wing defence and the centre, so that they can work together as a unit.

Defending in the Circle

When we look at specialising, defenders need to put in extra work to defend the circle, so the goal circle is an appropriate place to focus on as we look at the back third.

There are a number of ways to defend in the goal circle. Each relies on the ability of the two defenders to coordinate their movements and work in tandem. You can tell a good back line—its members work together to constantly pressure the shooters. Defenders who work in isolation make it easy for shooters to succeed.

One-on-One Defence

As previously discussed in Step 6, this term simply means taking responsibility for one player. In most instances it is a case of defending your opponent;

however, it is not limited to this. One-on-one defence can also include a deliberate switch of opponent, a tactic usually used within the goal circle, or a switch that occurs in the course of play. Each defender should be able to switch to defend the other shooter when necessary.

One-on-one defence means that a shooter is never left unattended in the goal circle. It is most effective against a balanced attack, when both shooters share the responsibilities for their team's score.

Double-Defence

As previously discussed in Step 8, in this play both defenders combine to pressure one shooter. The pressure from a double-defence should be strongest when the ball is passed into the goal circle so the shooter has to contest the catch against both defenders. The defenders should position themselves so they restrict the shooter's catching, passing and shooting options. One defender should be able to cut off the front ball, which is usually a flat or low ball, and the other should restrict the back ball, which is usually a high ball. Double-defence combinations can take a front and back starting position as close as possible to the shooter (see figure 9.1a), or offset a metre or so to either side of the shooter, while maintaining a front and back split (see figure 9.1b). The most common application of a double-defence in the circle is on a goal shooter who is obviously the opposition's key scorer.

Splitting the Circle

In this approach to defending the circle, defenders have clearly identified areas of responsibility. While defenders are aware of their opponents' moves, they do not chase the shooters within the goal circle. Instead, they focus on the ball which they attempt to intercept.

The defenders offset each other; one has responsibility for the front ball at the top of the goal circle, while the other for the back ball along the goal line (see figure 9.2). They constantly reposition as the ball comes down court, ensuring that they are well placed to intercept the pass in. They rely on players outside the circle to pressure the ball, as they have more chance of intercepting if balls are fed from a long way out. Balls fed from the edge of the circle are hard to intercept.

Figure 9.1a Double-defence in front and back positions.

Figure 9.1b Double-defence in offset positions.

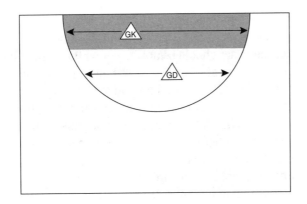

Figure 9.2 Splitting the goal circle.

Use this type of defence as a primary defence if both defenders have strong anticipation skills. It can, however, develop lazy defenders who are not prepared to do the hard chasing when needed. It is best to use "splitting the circle" defence intermittently as a strategy for unsettling an attacking rhythm.

Even after the best endeavour, defenders are still beaten within the circle. Make sure you do not give up at the point when the shooter takes aim. Remember, the harder you make life for shooters, the more likely you are to be successful, particularly in those all-important final minutes of a close contest. When you are beaten for the ball in the goal circle, recover quickly to defend the shot and then prepare to rebound.

Defending the Shot

In earlier times when shooters released the ball low from the shoulder, defenders with a strong jump took many balls out. Today shooters have a high release and defenders have to play it smart to extract a return from the defence of the shot. A varied defence is important—keep the shooter guessing. See if you can get shooters to focus on what you are doing rather than looking at the target, the goalpost. Now let us look at the two main ways of defending a shot: the lean and the jump.

The Lean

When the shooter takes possession of the ball, use the recovery step to move to the legal defending distance from the shooter's landed foot. Balance on either one foot or both and stretch forward to pressure the shot as close to the point of release as you can (see figure 9.3). Balancing on one foot allows

greater extension to the ball, while two feet gives you better body control. Using the arm opposite the leg you are standing on will maintain good extension and body control when executing the lean on one leg. Allow your body to "hang" in the space between you and your opponent. Be sure you don't lean over too far and over balance, as that can incur a penalty.

Most times you execute the lean in front of your opponent, but don't hesitate to try the side and back as starting positions for the lean. If the shot is close in, the back position can be a real nuisance to the shooters. Remember, variety is important.

The Jump

When you jump you are trying to deflect the shot. Recover to the legal distance as for the lean, but rather than stretching out, take a strong starting position (see figure 9.4). Crouch low beneath the shooter's immediate focus. Watch the shooter's hand. As the shooting action begins, uncoil like a tight spring. As the shooter releases the ball, propel yourself forward: aim to cut the shot off close to the point of release. Make sure you do not contact your opponent; that will incur a penalty.

Figure 9.3 Using the lean to pressure the shot.

Figure 9.4a Setting up for the jump to deflect a shot.

Figure 9.4b Upon release, propel yourself towards the ball, avoiding contact.

After you have defended the shot, prepare to rebound. Don't assume that the shot will score. Of course many do, but what you are waiting for are the missed goals. They are the ones that you can rebound and send down court for your team to score from.

Rebounding

Defenders should work together to rebound successfully. They should dictate the terms of the defence by working hard to establish strong rebounding positions. One defender should control the air, going after the ball, while the other controls the ground.

As the shooter begins the shooting motion, the defender controlling the ground should establish a strong rebounding position on the opposite side of the goalpost from the shooter. Take a position about half a step out from the goalpost, with your feet apart, body tense and holding space, and your eyes on the ball. Work to keep the shooter behind you. Use a rapid sidestep to protect your space if necessary. A strong rebounding position allows you to recover balls that come over your side of the ring.

As the shooter releases the shot both defenders turn towards the goalpost, drop their weight and prepare to rebound. Focus on the ball. As the ball hits the ring the defender who is covering that side uses a powerful explosive movement towards the ball. Reach out to take the ball at full extension. Remember, a one-handed take allows you greater extension. Pull the ball in quickly, cushion your landing and then send the ball safely down court. If you are unable to control the ball in the air, tap it to your partner waiting on the ground.

BACK THIRD

DRILLS

The drills presented here are structured to enable you to build a repertoire of specialised defending skills through well-planned challenges. Begin with the basics and as you handle them confidently, progress to the more challenging drills. Remember, it is better to develop one skill really well in a session than to simply go through the motions with all of them.

1. Circle Practice

Begin with one defender and one shooter in the circle. The second shooter and defender work outside the circle. Shooters pass three times to each other before putting up a shot. Defenders work to cause a breakdown of the attacking play, to tip, or to intercept the ball. When this occurs the two groups change working areas.

Success Goal = Each defender causes a breakdown before the shooter takes a shot ___

Success Check
• Watch ball and opponent ___
• Control body movements ___
• Attack the ball ___
• Apply pressure ___

To Increase Difficulty
• Both shooters and defenders work within the circle. The wing attack and wing defence operate outside.
• Finally, add the centre players to the outside team.

To Decrease Difficulty
• Increase the number of passes between attackers to five before the shot can go up.

2. Double-Defence

One shooter and two defenders are in the circle. The defenders position for a double-defence of the shooter. Two undefended attackers are outside the circle with the ball. Starting from the transverse line they pass the ball between themselves for up to five passes, watching for the best pass into the circle. Defenders constantly reposition to ensure both can contest the ball when it comes in.

Success Goal = A defender takes possession of the ball passed in to the goal shooter ___

Success Check
• Position to cut off pass ___
• Both defenders contest the pass ___
• Work together to deny the shooter possession ___

To Increase Difficulty
• Allow the second shooter to enter the circle.
• Add the centre to the attacking team.

3. Splitting the Goal Circle

Defenders use an offset defence in the circle. They position on either side of the goalpost: one forward for the front ball, and one along the goal line to cover the long pass. One shooter is in the circle, the other is working the outside. Defenders position to cover their areas on either side of the goalpost. The shooters pass freely to each other as they move around the area. The defenders concentrate on cutting off passes to the shooter in the circle. Only one shooter is in the circle at any time.

 ***Success Goal*** = Defenders successfully tip or intercept 3 passes ___

✔ **Success Check**
• Constantly reposition ___
• Focus on the ball ___
• Keep the passing options covered ___
• Watch for the intercept ___
• Commit to the take ___

To Increase Difficulty
• The two shooters work in the circle. Add the wing attack and wing defence outside the circle.
• When the success goal is reached, add both centre players outside the circle.

4. Tough Work

Two shooters are in the circle with the ball. They move freely about the circle, passing the ball to themselves. The shooter who receives the fifth pass takes the shot. One defender works in the circle trying to take the ball from the shooters before the shot goes up. When a defender is successful, she or he earns a rest and is replaced by a partner.

Success Goal = Intercept the ball before the shot goes up ___

✔ **Success Check**
• Know where both shooters are ___
• Be aware of the ball ___
• Apply pressure selectively ___
• Work to establish a successful option ___

To Increase Difficulty
• The defender now must defend the shot and rebound.
• Add all outside players.

5. Defending the Shot

One shooter and one defender are in the circle, and a feeder is on the outside with the ball. The feeder calls "go" and the shooter offers. The defender allows the shooter to take the ball. The defender applies a defence to the shot and rebounds.

Success Goal = Defender's pressure causes an unsuccessful shot ____

Success Check
- Watch ball as you recover ____
- Start in a strong position ____
- Pressure release of shot ____
- Block shooter's run to the goalpost after they shoot ____

To Increase Difficulty
- Pressure the shooter's move, then defend the shot and rebound.

6. Wall Rebounding

Place a cone next to the practice wall. Mark a cross on the wall at goalpost height (10 feet/3.05 metres) directly above the cone. Stand facing the wall and throw the ball to the target on the wall. Jump strongly to pull the ball in. Make sure you do not contact the cone while in the air or on landing. Absorb the impact of landing by bending your knees when you contact the ground. Remember, a two-handed pull gives you the best control over the ball. A one-handed take provides better elevation. Practice both.

Success Goal = 5 consecutive successful rebounds ____

Success Check
- Strong low base ____
- Elevate quickly ____
- Take ball at full stretch ____

To Increase Difficulty
- Turn sideways to start the practice.
- Now try the opposite side.
- Contest the drill with a partner.

7. Goalpost Rebounding

When you practice rebounding at the goalpost, you work in match-like conditions. Begin the work alone. As your confidence and skill level increase, introduce an opponent and then your defending partner and their opponent. The drills listed below will enable you to have good body control when you try those strong jumps. It will also help time your move precisely.

a. Feeder stands behind the goalpost. The rebounder is on court, half a stride out from the post, with eyes on the goal ring. The feeder throws the ball onto the goal ring. As it hits the ring, elevate strongly to take the ball as close to the goalpost ring as possible.

b. Stretch elastic straps across the top of the goal ring so the ball rebounds from every shot. Work the drill for defence of the shot with the straps across the ring.

Success Goal = 5 consecutive successful rebounds ___

Success Check
- Establish your starting position ___
- Lower weight for strong take-off ___
- Drive body straight to ball ___
- Take ball at maximum extension ___
- Absorb impact of landing ___

To Increase Difficulty
- Contest the rebound with a partner.
- Include another two rebounders in the drill. This allows the two defenders to work as a team. One should be airborne while the other controls the ground.
- Add the outside players so that the ball can be passed out of the defence third when the defenders win the rebound.

8. Outside Defence

The wing attack has the ball at the transverse line and the wing defence is pressuring the pass. Both centres are in the centre third about three metres from the transverse line. Wing attack calls "go". The attacking centre drives into the goal third to take the pass. The wing attack and centre must work the ball to the circle's edge. The centre and wing defence defend every move and try to stop their opponent from landing at the circle's edge with the ball.

Success Goal = 3 successful defences by the outside players that stop the attack from reaching the circle ___

To Increase Difficulty
- Place one shooter in the circle and allow that player to come out to assist the attack.

Success Check
- Be aware of partner ___
- Use voice to direct if necessary ___
- Maintain pressure ___
- Back your judgement—intercept ___

BACK THIRD SUCCESS SUMMARY

If you are playing in the back third of the netball court, your main role is to defend. In your specialist session you should hone these skills. This will enable you to increase your effectiveness on court. To be successful, the players in the back third need to work together to offer a strong varied defence every time the opposition takes the ball towards their goal. Being able to play one-on-one, split the circle and double-defend in the circle makes it difficult for your opponents to score. You exert even more pressure if you defend the shot and develop a strong rebound. The outside players must work hard too. If they can hold the ball up it enhances the circle defenders' chance for success.

STEP 10

THE CENTRE THIRD: LINKING DEFENCE AND ATTACK

N etball starts in the centre third. The centre pass starts each quarter of a match and restarts the game when a goal has been scored. The other major role of the centre third is to link the team's attacking and defending ends. Specialist work for mid-court players should heighten awareness of these roles and develop skills that enable them to perform effectively on court

When you look at mid-court play you must remember the goal attack and goal defence. While essentially their roles specialise in the front or back thirds, they still need to participate in some parts of training for mid-court specialisation: perhaps the final 15 minutes of a session.

Why Is Specialising in the Centre Third Important?

Being able to win your centre pass gives you a great advantage in attack. Sending the ball confidently and quickly out of the centre and into your attacking third towards your goal pressures your opponents. Defenders have difficulty containing free-flowing attacks.

To win the centre pass your team needs to have well-laid plans that you can execute efficiently. Your team is given every second centre pass, and you need to use it well. When the ball comes out of the centre third with planned precision, the shooters waiting behind to execute their moves can feel the confidence. It creates a very positive environment for your team.

The reverse is also true. When a team struggles to take the ball out of the centre third, the attack end struggles to create a flow. It is therefore important that your team can also defend the centre pass and try to slow the pace of the opposition's attack. To force the error and gain a turnover is great play.

The other important role of the mid-court is to link the back and front thirds: the defending specialists with the shooters. When the ball comes out of the back third your opponents have lost their opportunity to score—your team is now in a position to gain an advantage. The mid-court players must work the ball safely through their area so your team has a chance to score and capitalise on the good work of the back line.

Starting: The Centre Pass

The captain's toss decides who takes the first centre pass. The winner has the choice of the centre pass or selecting the team's shooting end. It is quite rare for the winner to give possession of the ball away. It is a definite advantage to win the toss and get the first score on the board.

Consistently winning your centre pass—passing it successfully into your attacking third—is what good netball teams train to do. Your team's aim should be to win all of their centre passes and then to capture a few from the opposition each quarter—a very simple and effective philosophy that is emphasised from schooldays to representative matches. Your team is given every other centre pass, which gives you as many opportunities for success as your opponents; the trick is to tip the advantage your way by intercepting some of their passes.

All of this goes to reinforce the importance of the centre pass and the need to provide specialised sessions on which to work during your training time. Your team needs a number of well-understood options to ensure that they can consistently win the centre pass.

Winning the Centre Pass

As with other netball strategies, to win the centre pass your team must be organised. There are four team members who can offer moves. If all four offer simultaneously, then two or three moves will probably be wasted. There is also a restricted amount of court space available, so staggering the offers is much more effective.

The first offer should come strongly as the whistle blows. The player offering should drive hard and fast to an open space. The centre concentrates on this offer and determines if it is, or is not, realistic (about two seconds). The other three players prepare or begin to execute their offers by reading from the first player. If the move is successful, then they do not need to offer any backup. If this is not the case, then they must quickly offer alternative moves. Remember, you have only three seconds from the whistle to get the ball away.

The following plays illustrate some options for winning the centre pass.

The Wing Attack Has the Line

As the wing attack, you take the pivotal role and provide the first option. Move to the centre of the transverse line. As your centre prepares to enter the centre circle, offer a strong preliminary move. This draws the defence prior to the whistle. Remember: a well-executed preliminary move sends the defender in one direction while you make your offer in the other. You may recall that this move was covered in Step 5. As the centre enters the centre circle the whistle blows. This is the cue for you to put a strong offer out: to drive hard over the line and take the ball (see figure 10.1).

The wing defence and goal defence are your backup players. If your initial move is not strong, they follow quickly from the back transverse line. One drives close to the centre to take a straight pass, while the other stays wide to take a high ball. The goal attack produces a clearing move to the side of the court. As soon as the centre pass is taken, the goal attack provides the first offer to pull the ball into the attacking third.

Using a Split

Wing attack and goal attack start from the middle of their transverse line. They move on the spot, one in

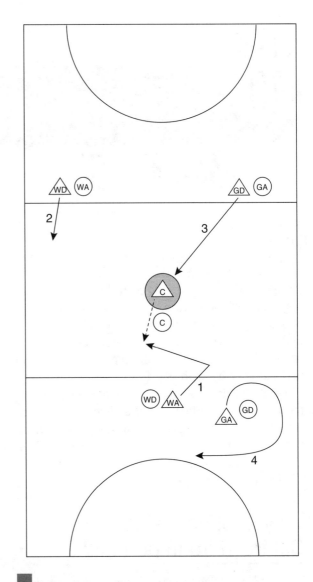

Figure 10.1 The wing attack has the line.

front of the other, as the centre prepares to pass. As the whistle sounds both players offer, driving strongly in opposite directions. The centre passes to the best lead. Wing defence and goal defence offer backup leads after one second if it appears neither of the first leads will be used (see figure 10.2).

The Wide Start

Wing attack and goal attack are on their transverse line, well apart from each other. They hold their positions on the line so one can cut to the centre and one can offer wide on the opposite side. As the whistle sounds, the short offer comes first over the line, quickly followed by the other offer heading down court. Again, the goal defence and wing

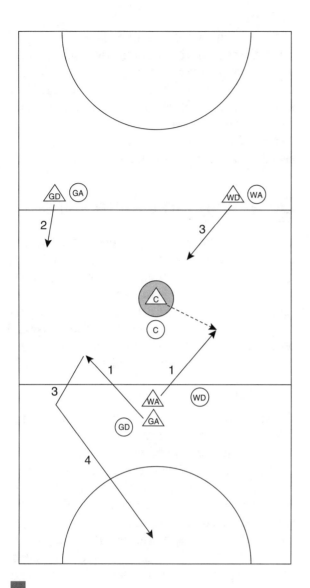

Figure 10.2 Using a split.

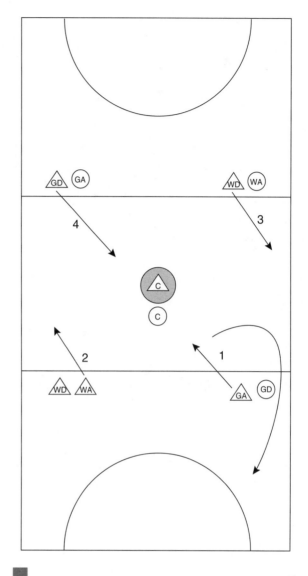

Figure 10.3 The wide start.

defence act as backup players if they feel the two attackers are struggling to pull the ball through (see figure 10.3).

The Back Door

All four players are at their transverse lines. The attackers move behind their line looking as though they will offer. The opposition cannot read that the first move is about to come from the wing defence. Wing defence drives to the open space and calls to the centre. The goal defence offers the second move, while the wing attack provides the backup if necessary. The goal attack drives hard to the circle, which allows the goal shooter to take the first ball into the attacking third (see figure 10.4).

Centre pass play calls for you to be creative and there are many options that you can employ. The important point is to ensure you have variety and understanding; you must know the order of the offers. It is fun to develop code words that signal to your team members just what the play will be. This is very helpful for young players, and one of the easiest ways is to use numbers. One means wing attack, two means back door, which means either the wing defence or the goal defence. Another approach is to use key words: drive means wing attack, sprint means split. Of course it does not take your opposition long to figure out just what you are calling, so it's a good idea to change the words every quarter. This tests your concentration too!

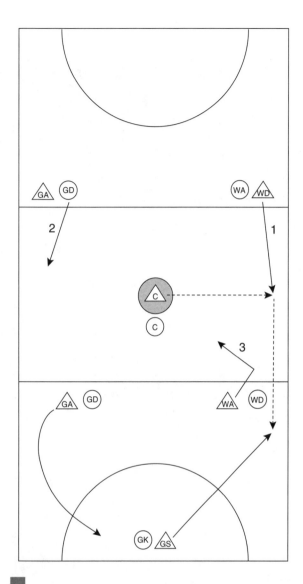

Figure 10.4 The back door.

Some teams use their centre player to signal the order of play. If the ball is on the right side it means wing attack will offer first; on the left, the back door, the wing defence or goal defence will offer first. The more experienced players use their eyes to read the moves and use their voice only when needed. For the young or inexperienced, it is both fun and useful to signal or call centre pass moves.

Defending the Centre Pass

While your team has every second centre pass to attack from, it also has to defend every other centre pass. Remember this equation when you are organising your training time. Ensure that you spend equal amounts of time defending and attacking the centre pass. Some teams enjoy the attacking play and practice this almost to the exclusion of defence. Do not make this mistake. Keep good balance in your work.

The Double-Defence

Use your numbers to your advantage. This form of defence works well when your opponents are obviously sending their centre passes through one player. Use your centre to double up your defence on that player (usually the wing attack), to try to cause an error (see figure 10.5). What you are endeavouring to train is good decision making by the athletes who are applying the double-defence. There is a point in time when the double needs to be taken off; that is, it is no longer applied or you may well disadvantage

Figure 10.5 Double up defenders on key players to help you win the centre pass.

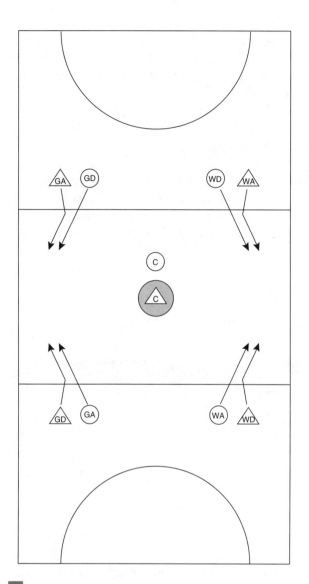

Figure 10.6 By limiting attacking players' movements, you force the centre to be accurate.

Figure 10.7 Using a wide stance to pressure the centre pass.

Pressure the Pass

No matter how well you defend the passing options, if the straight line between your opponents is not pressured then you will find it difficult to be successful: to intercept the ball or cause an attacking error to occur. As centre you concentrate on your opponent. Stand the legal distance from the centre circle, drop your weight, and adopt a strong and imposing stance that protects the centre passing lane (see figure 10.7). Spread your arms wide to pressure the release.

Linking Attack and Defence

The other major role of the mid-court is to link the team's attacking and defending play. In attack you aim to create a smooth transition from the back third to the front third. If the ball travels quickly down court, the attackers find it easier to keep the flow going. Shooters can find it difficult to time their moves accurately if the ball is stopping and starting on its way through the mid-court.

In defence it is important to maintain pressure on your opponents. It is very difficult for the defenders to operate successfully if their mid-court players allow the ball to travel rapidly down court. Remember, a turnover in your team's mid-court is that much closer to your own goal than one obtained in the back third.

your team's next attacking move. For example, your opposing centre will be allowed to drive to her or his goal circle undefended. Work to find the balance here and seek input from the coach and players.

Dictating the Line of Attack

Work hard before the whistle blows to hold a strong starting position on the line. You should try to limit the attacker's options. Force the attacker wide to the side of the court. Make sure you are on the inside so the ball has to pass you to reach your opponent (see figure 10.6). If the centre does not throw with great accuracy, you have a good chance to force mistakes.

Operating Effectively Around the Goal Circle

The centre, wing attack and wing defence are all restricted from entering the goal circle during match play. They need to develop an awareness of the circle and be adept at working effectively around it. Remember, players who go offside (enter the goal circle) are penalised.

Although the goal circle is not a part of the playing area of the mid-court, it is a common playing area for the centre, wing attack and wing defence. For this reason these drills are included in this step rather than with the front or back third. In a special-ist session, take time to develop awareness and balance around the goal circle. It is best to do this work in two- or three-minute slots between very demanding work.

Many netballers feel they are best balanced on the goal circle when they are at full stretch on one leg, like a lunge. In fact your body is better balanced on a wide base, with both feet on the ground. Use this stance as your starting point around the circle. Remember, a strong base not only keeps you well balanced, it also enables you to generate a powerful take-off if you need to quickly move away from the circle.

CENTRE THIRD

DRILLS

As a mid-court specialist you need good balance between your attacking and defending skills: alternate your role at each centre pass. In general court play you must also react quickly to a turnover by changing from attack to defence or vice versa. The drills in this section are designed to develop this ability and to help you create winning moves for your centre pass.

1. Centre Release

The ability of the centre to release the pass accurately is very important for success at the centre pass. This drill overloads the centre line to really challenge the centre's ability to release the ball accurately under pressure. Three attackers are on the transverse line in the front third and one defender is in the centre third. The centre is outside the centre circle with the ball and the coach stands behind her or him. The centre steps into the centre circle. The whistle is blown by the coach, and all three attackers offer. Centre selects the most appropriate option and passes accurately. Coach assesses and discusses the choice with the centre.

Success Goal = 3 consecutive successful centre passes ___

Success Check
• See all moves ___
• Select the best option ___
• Narrow your focus ___
• Release the pass quickly ___

To Increase Difficulty
• Add a second defender to the centre third.
• Add a third defender to the centre third.

To Decrease Difficulty
• Begin with only two attackers and after reaching the success goal increase the number of attackers to three.

2. Holding on the Line

As the defending player, position yourself on the transverse line to force your opponent wide for the centre pass. Your attacking opponent has two seconds to try to reposition on your inside. Neither player can enter the centre third or cause contact. You will find in match play that you frequently need to reposition at the centre pass. As previously discussed in Step 5, the hold is a very useful move to protect space.

Success Goal = Hold the line position 3 times consecutively ___

Success Check
• Weight down, strong starting position ___
• Work feet and legs across your space ___
• Watch opponent and the ball ___

To Increase Difficulty
• After two seconds blow the whistle for a centre pass. Defender now contests the take with the opponent.

3. Evens

As the attacker, you stand at the transverse line with your defending player beside you. Hold your position strongly to protect the most direct line between you and your team's centre. The centre has the ball and when she or he steps into the circle the whistle sounds. This is your cue to drive forward to take the pass. If you hold your space well you should just outrun your opponent. If you have not held space well, revise the move in Step 5.

Success Goal = 3 consecutive successful centre passes ___

Success Check
• Weight down ___
• Hold your space ___
• Eyes on ball ___
• React on whistle ___

To Increase Difficulty
• Add another attacking or defending combination to the transverse line. Both attackers offer on the whistle.

4. Beating the Double

As the name implies, this drill looks at how to create winning attacking moves to beat a double-defence at the centre pass. Stand a metre back from the transverse line. One defender is with you, the other is immediately in front over the transverse line. The centre stands outside the circle with the ball. As the centre steps forward into the circle to start the drill, you offer a strong preliminary move to spilt the defenders and create space in which to work. As the whistle blows to start play, drive hard over the line to take the centre pass.

All players who contest the centre pass should practice against the double-defence—it can be applied to any of them. In reality, the wing attack probably contests the double-defence more than the other players combined, so give the wing attack every second set of centre passes.

Success Goal = 2 successful centre passes where you beat a double-defence ____

Success Check
- Weight down to generate power ____
- Work effectively before the whistle ____
- Watch the ball ____
- React to cues ____
- Fully extend to take the ball ____

To Increase Difficulty
- Try to beat the double without using a preliminary move. Simply outrun or outjump both players.
- The goal attack and goal defence join the drill.

5. Double-Defence

Here are two drills to help you develop skills you can use to apply a successful double-defence at the centre pass.

a. The two defending players work together. As one of the defenders, you are behind the transverse line. Position yourself to direct the attacker wide. Your centre covers your opponent as she or he crosses the line. Both defending players maintain pressure until the catch is taken.

b. Introduce the other centre-third players but maintain the double-defence on the wing attack. Allow any other attacker to take the centre pass. The attackers will then pass the ball down court towards their goal until they have made two passes in this attacking third. This requires the wing defence and centre to effectively cover their players after applying the double-defence. It is important that the opposition's centre is not given free rein to enter the attacking third from the centre pass. This can happen when a double-defence is used.

Success Goal =
a. Intercept or disrupt 2 centre passes ____
b. Intercept or disrupt 2 passes in the back third ____

Success Check
- Position early ____
- Work together ____
- Communicate your movements ____
- Watch the player and the ball ____

6. Linking Attack

The five attacking mid-court players are on court as shown (see figure). The thrower stands in the back third with the ball. To start the drill, the thrower passes the ball into the back third. The player nearest to the ball drives hard to gain possession, then passes the ball to the next player who offers a strong move. This player then passes to the next and so on. Players look for space to offer their moves and time their moves well so their leads can be used. All attackers work at these skills to enable the ball to travel quickly through the centre third. After the ball has crossed into the front third, the thrower releases the next ball and the drill begins again.

Success Goal = The ball successfully moves quickly and smoothly to link the back third and front third on 3 consecutive plays ___

Success Check
- Attackers react quickly ___
- Read moves from each other ___
- Offer strongly to open space ___
- Watch ball ___
- Pass accurately ___

To Increase Difficulty
- Thrower begins play with a sideline throw in in the back third.
- Place two defenders in the mid-court to pressure the attackers as the ball comes through.
- Each time you reach the success goal, add another defender until all players have an opponent.

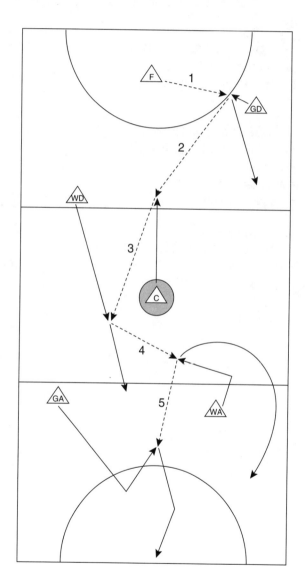

7. Linking Defence

This drill really works the first linking drill in reverse. The five mid-court players assume a defending role and the four attackers are on court opposing them. The thrower is in the front third with the ball. To start the drill, the thrower passes to the nearest attacker. This pass is the cue for defenders closest to the ball to apply pressure. Defenders should cover offers, contest the pass and recover to defend the pass if they cannot intercept the first ball.

The defenders apply full pressure to each pass as the attackers try to work the ball through the mid-court. After the defenders are successful (they cause a breakdown: an intercept, a deflection, or a poor attacking pass) return the ball to the thrower who restarts the drill.

Success Goal = To link the defending play of the team to cause 3 breakdowns from your opponent's attacking play ___

Success Check

• Defenders work together ___
• Communicate ___
• Maintain pressure ___
• All players contribute ___

To Increase Difficulty

• Thrower starts the play from a sideline throw in in the attacking third.
• Add another attacker so all players have an opponent.

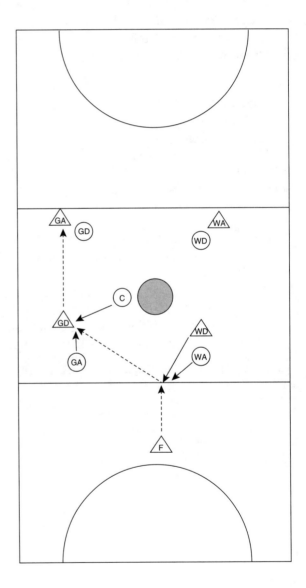

8. Shooters Out

Two teams line up on court without their shooters. In this drill the goal keepers simply start or end the passage of play and are stationary at the top of their goal circle. The drill practices linking in very match-like conditions, which requires players to rapidly switch from attack to defence. When your team has possession of the ball, it is in attack; the reverse also applies.

Your team has won the toss. Your goal keeper has the ball and your team is in attack. You try to pass the ball down court to the opposition's goal keeper. The team must handle the ball in each third before passing it to the goal keeper. If you achieve this you score one point. Your opponent's goal keeper then sends the ball into attack for the other team. You are now in defence.

If your team loses possession as the ball comes down court, you simply play on. You must quickly change to defence and try to win it back. Each time the ball is passed to the opposition's goal keeper, the team scores a point. Normal match play rules apply.

Success Goal = First team to score 5 points wins ___

Success Check
• Adjust rapidly ___
• Work with team-mates ___
• Communicate with each other ___

To Increase Difficulty
• A team must make a minimum of two passes in each third before passing the ball to their opponent's goal keeper.

9. Balance Catches

These practices will assist the centre, wing attack, and wing defence in moving confidently around the edge of the goal circle.

a. Stand on the circle's edge, facing the goalpost. Drop your weight. The thrower stands two steps in front of you. The thrower releases 10 quick passes at varying heights. You must quickly retrieve each ball and return it to the thrower without leaving the circle's edge and without overbalancing into the goal circle. The thrower should pass the ball so you can extend forward to take the ball and confine sideways movement to one step. It is important to make quick accurate reactions.

b. Introduce a partner to contest the balls. The wide base is now even more important to hold your position on the edge of the circle. Make sure the thrower places the ball so both players can contest fairly.

c. Now combine this work with some fast movements. At the beginning it is good to maintain your balance while you are stationary, but in match play you need to do this with movement. Work through the sequence above using a mobile start. Move three to four strides away from the circle. Drive hard onto the edge of the circle, then quickly work the drill as before.

Success Goal =

a. 10 balls taken consecutively without leaving the edge of the circle or falling into the circle ____

b. 5 balls taken consecutively without leaving the edge of the circle or falling into the circle ____

c. 10 and then 5 balls taken consecutively without leaving the edge of the circle or falling into the circle ____

To Increase Difficulty

- Reverse your starting position and back onto the circle. Thrower is front of you.
- Turn onto the right side and repeat the drill. Then work from your left side.

Success Check

- React quickly ____
- Focus on ball ____
- Keep weight low ____
- Attack ball, reach out for it ____

10. Find the Edge

This drill helps with your goal circle awareness. Stand two steps away from the circle and focus on the line that marks the circle. Close your eyes. Move forward quickly to the line. Open your eyes. Are you there?

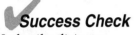

Success Goal = Land accurately on the line twice from 3 attempts ____

Success Check
- Judge the distance ____
- Visualise the distance ____
- Move confidently ____
- Move on the edge ____

To Increase Difficulty
- Stand on the edge of the circle facing the goalpost. Shuffle right three steps quickly with your eyes closed. Are you still on the circle?
- Shuffle left three steps. Are you still there?
- Now reverse your starting position and repeat the drill.

CENTRE THIRD SUCCESS SUMMARY

As a mid-court player you have the key to the team's start. Your task is to win the centre pass and to make it as difficult as you can for your opponents to win theirs. You must be a pivotal player in linking the defence and attack ends of your team, and you should know just where that goal circle is. It is a demanding role. You will run all day, constantly changing from attack to defence. Your team has every chance for success if you play your part well.

STEP 11

THE FRONT THIRD: SCORING FROM THE ATTACK

It is exciting to play in the front third. You have the chance to put the finishing touches on your team's down-court play, whether it's by placing one of those really delicate passes on the fingertips of your shooters, or actually putting the ball through the ring and scoring a goal.

Shooting is obviously an important factor in the success of the front third. Good conversion rates are important for winning netball. As the skill of shooting was covered in Step 4, this step looks at the other on-court skills that are necessary for the front third to function well. Remember, the attacking third is not only about shooters. Although they are no doubt the focus, it is important that all four players work together effectively to create the highest number of scoring opportunities for your team.

Why Is Specialising in the Front Third Important?

The key function of the front third of the court is to attack—to deliver the ball safely to the team's shooters who convert a high percentage of shots to goals. Scoring more goals than your opponent wins netball matches.

The hallmark of successful attack work is organisation. In a sport that requires you to make accurate split-second decisions, a basic plan is essential. It helps all athletes to understand their role and enables them to more accurately time their movements. Of course, drilling teams to the point where they are mechanical is not the answer either. The plan should provide the basic framework that is embellished by individual interpretation and ability. A healthy balance between order and flair creates an exciting, winning attack.

Organising the Attack Third

Given the importance of the shooters—they are the only people who can score—it is sensible to adopt a philosophy that has the other team members responsible for bringing the ball down the court to them. You really don't want to see the goal attack become the dominant centre-court player. Others can fulfil that role. The goal attack needs to be most effective in her or his area of specialisation: the front third.

This thinking holds that one shooter should always be at home, in the goal circle, ready to take any ball that a team member decides is safe to pass in. It is interesting to note how often a surprise long ball from the centre third that is passed straight into the goal circle can find its mark.

There's no doubt that the safest feed into the circle comes from a player on the circle's edge passing to one shooter held by one defender. This is a very difficult situation for a defender. Only those with outstanding skill can beat these odds.

However, if the attacking team continually works one play, the predictability diminishes its chances for success. In attack it is important to develop variety, which allows you to maintain possession. One way to do this is to organise the offers and to have a plan for the front end that clearly identifies the role of the shooters during match play. There are many ways to achieve this. Here are a few examples.

Shooter Has the Circle

Your team has a dominant goal shooter whom you let work the circle. The goal attack, wing attack and centre do all the attack work outside the circle. They combine well to deliver the ball to the goal shooter. The goal attack enters the circle late, preferably when the goal shooter has the ball. Both are ready to contest any rebound, but still expects to contribute significantly to the team's score. When the team gives the goal shooter the circle, there is a high expectation that that player will offer strongly and shoot accurately.

Shooters Alternate the Lead

The shooter who has the lead takes the first ball that comes into the front third. If needed that player drives hard up to the transverse line to pull the ball into the front third. The other shooter works in the goal circle. One shooter calls for the lead to change. This usually occurs as the ball is returned to the centre after a goal has been scored. The shooters reverse roles until the lead changes again.

This tactic works well when both shooters are mobile players who can share the shooting and playing workload. Wing attack and centre play a secondary role, reading their moves from the shooters. They wait for a shooter to commit to a space before they offer. This avoids the problem of the outside feeder and a shooter heading for the same court space.

Shooters Are Playing Deep

The shooters are operating in the back half of the attacking third (towards the goal line). They wait for the wing attack and centre to work the ball into the front third before they begin to offer. The goal attack usually takes the first pass from the feeding players and then tries to pass it directly to the goal shooter (see figure 11.1). This play works well where shooters can work together as a unit; it does not demand the mobility needed to alternate the lead.

The Circle Is Closed

Both shooters operate in the circle; neither moves outside to take a pass. They wait patiently for the ball to be brought down court by other team members. Once the ball is on the edge of the circle they offer strongly and try to take the ball in a good shooting position. This allows them to go straight to the goalpost, to take a shot at the goal.

This play allows the shooters to concentrate on scoring, as they are only required to give one lead. Both shooters need to be adept at working in the circle at one time. With their two defenders also present, space is limited. For the goal shooter, holding your position becomes a key factor for success.

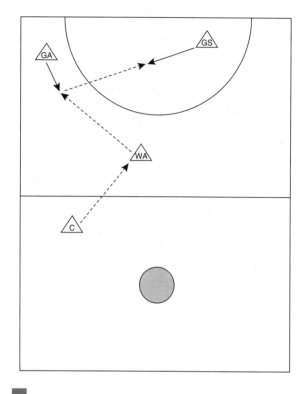

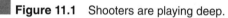 **Figure 11.1** Shooters are playing deep.

Other team members need to work harder on the down-court attack when the circle is closed. In particular the wing defence and goal defence must follow through the full centre third and stay on the transverse line to back up the front-third attack.

The Lead Is Split

The goal shooter leads to balls that enter the front third from the left-hand side of the court as you look to the centre third. The goal attack leads to balls that come down the right-hand side. The shooter that does not lead is in the goal circle ready to take any ball that is passed in. When the leading shooter has taken the ball, she or he plays it onto the other shooter or to the feeders, then drives hard into the circle. It is important to make sure the entry does not cut across another team member's path, particularly the shooting partner.

This is an easy way to sort the attack when you have two mobile shooters who are accurate and enjoy sharing the workload.

The Double-Play

One of the shooters has the lead and drives out to take the ball as it enters the front third. The shooting partner prepares to offer in the circle. The leading shooter passes to one of the feeders, who attempts to take the ball close to the circle's edge. The feeder looks to the circle as if to pass to the shooter inside. This shooter uses a clearing run to exit the circle. The leading shooter enters the circle and drives hard to the goalpost to complete the double-play (see figure 11.2).

This is a good change of tactic best employed when the shooter on the lead has quite clearly lost her or his defender. This play allows you to drive home the momentum established outside the circle.

These are a few ideas for organising the attack; there are many more. You will enjoy planning your attacking moves and working out ways to communicate the play. Some teams use numbers, some names.

Good attacking ends are organised and very skilful at changing their play at appropriate times. Don't wait until your moves have totally broken down before changing your pattern of play. Develop a feel for this. When you see the signs that your opponents have caught on to your strategy, change quickly to another pattern.

Throw Ins

The wing attack or centre should take throw ins that are in the attacking third and outside of the goal circle. This allows the attack to operate with both shooters able to offer. If you use a shooter to throw in outside the circle, you unnecessarily limit your team's options for attack. As the on-court feeder is often under double-defence, a clever tactic for this player is to use a clearing run to draw both the wing defence and centre away from the intended pass. This creates a space for one of the shooters to work in.

Rebounds

Shooters should be able to contest the rebound successfully: it means goals. The shooter who is not taking aim should move quickly to the goalpost to cover the opposite side of the ring to the shooting partner. The ideal position is about half a step from the goalpost, feet at a wide stance, weight down, and eyes focused on the ball.

As the shot is released, turn to the post and watch the flight of the ball to the ring. If it is unsuccessful, jump strongly into the air to take possession, or tap the ball to your shooting partner. The shooter who has executed the shot should follow their shot to the post and also contest the rebound. The rebound drills previously described in Step 9 provide good practice for you.

You are well equipped in the front third if you have three or four plays that your team can switch between. Keep the play consistent whether you are operating from a centre pass, turnover or throw in.

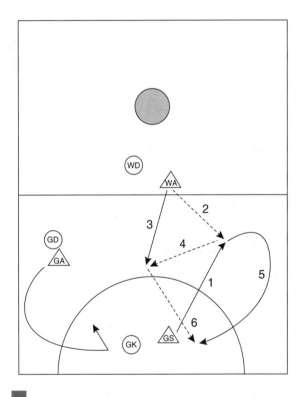

Figure 11.2 The double play.

ATTACKING THIRD

DRILLS

It is important that the shooters can work the circle together: that they have a feel for each other's movements and work in harmony. Your feeders (wing attack and centre) must be able to pass the ball to shooters with pinpoint accuracy. The drills in this chapter are designed to assist you in developing these important skills. They start with simple tasks and limited defence. As your skill level and confidence rise, the defence increases to test your skills under match-like conditions.

1. Goal Circle Awareness

Both shooters are in the circle. The feeders (wing attack and centre) are on the outside with the ball. To start the drill, both shooters move freely within the circle. The feeders and shooters pass the ball from the outside to the inside of the goal circle and then back out again. After the ball enters the circle for the third time the shooter takes a shot.

Success Goal = 5 successful passes and 1 goal ____

Success Check
- Move to space ____
- Pass to space ____
- Focus on ball ____
- Be aware of other players ____

To Increase Difficulty
- Add a defender to the inside of the circle.
- Add 2 defenders and reduce the success goal to 3 passes and 1 goal.
- Add the wing defence and centre outside the circle and keep the success goal at 3 passes and 1 goal.

To Decrease Difficulty
- Reduce the number of successful passes to 3 and build up by two.

2. Goal Circle Re-entry

A shooter and defender are inside the goal circle. The feeder (wing attack or centre) is a few steps inside the transverse line of the attacking third. The shooter leads out to take a pass from the feeder, which the defender allows the shooter to take. The defender then applies strong defence to the shooter's path to the circle. The feeder drives to edge of circle. The shooter passes to the feeder, then attempts to beat the defence and take the ball in the circle and score a goal.

Success Goal = 3 successful goals scored from three re-entered drills ___

Success Check

- Attack strongly ___
- Watch ball ___
- Be aware of defender ___
- Create space; work in it ___

To Increase Difficulty

- Add another defender to defend the feeder or double-defend the shooter.
- The second shooter and defender now come on court. The shooter who is in the circle can offer alternative moves after the lead shooter has taken the first ball. The shooter outside the circle must be aware of the space in which the circle shooter needs to work. Make sure you do not cut across this player's path as you re-enter the goal circle.

To Decrease Difficulty

- Allow the defender to float between the leading shooter and the feeder. Once the shooter begins to re-enter with confidence, work the drill as above.

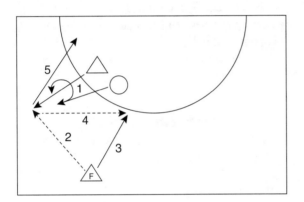

3. Organising the Lead

This drill provides the opportunity for you, the shooter, to organise the lead. You communicate the play to your attacking team members who are on court as shown. Two defenders apply pressure in the attacking third; they are not marking specific players. They offer a floating defence and attempt to run and intercept loose balls. To start the drill, the centre throws the ball into the air then catches it. Your attack responds as planned to bring the ball down court for a shot at goal.

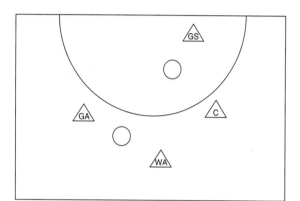

Success Goal = 2 goals scored from the planned attacking play ___

To Increase Difficulty

- After achieving the success goal, goal shooter calls for players to use a different lead. Continue in this manner until you have worked three or four lead changes.
- If you have a play that your team really wants to use more frequently than the others, then allow the goal shooter to call for this lead every other change.
- Add a third defender and allow the defending players to begin to offer some one-on-one defence as well as some floating defence.
- Add the fourth defender and give full-pressure defence to the attackers.
- If you need extra pressure, introduce a fifth defender to really target a specific attacker or to float between players. In this case, change the success goal to 1 goal.

4. Edging Closer

This drill assists the shooter who has a long shot from the outer perimeter of the circle to gain a closer shot.

a. The shooter is in the shooting position facing the goalpost, a step or two inside the circle. A feeder (wing attack or centre) is on the circle edge behind the shooter, just to the side of their shooting arm. The shooter takes aim, then quickly pulls the ball down, turns toward the feeder, and flicks a quick pass. At the same time the shooter quickly moves her or his back foot closer to the post. The feeder flicks the ball back to shooter, who quickly turns and faces the goalpost again. To be effective, the ball and players must move with speed.

b. Add a defender to the drill to defend the shot. The shooters must make sure they do not contact the defenders as they step closer to the goalpost. It is best to slide your foot quickly towards the goalpost and then transfer your weight to both feet as you regain your stance.

Success Goal = Gain a step closer to the goalpost and score a goal ___

Success Check
• Make the move a surprise ___
• Pass quickly ___
• Step quickly ___
• Recover and focus for shot ___

5. Two in the Circle

The two shooters and their defenders are in the goal circle. The feeders (wing attack and centre) are on the circle's edge, and one has the ball. To start the drill the feeders must pass between themselves before passing the ball into the goal circle. Feeders and shooters are moving, space is at a premium. Make sure you use it well and that passes are made with pinpoint accuracy. The shooter then catches the ball and shoots for goal.

Success Goal = 1 successful goal at the end of the passing task ___

Success Check
• Pass accurately ___
• Move into space ___
• Keep variety in the pass ___
• Control the shot ___

To Increase Difficulty
• Shooters and feeders must make four passes before taking the shot.
• Add the two defending players to the outside of the circle.

To Decrease Difficulty
• Begin with only one defender in the circle. Add the second defender as the attack's confidence grows.

6. By the Post

This drill practices the throw in from the back of the goal circle (goal line). As either shooter can take the pass, both should do so in practice. Both defenders defend the shooter in the circle. The wing attack and centre are well balanced on the edge of the circle. They are strategically placed on either side of the goal circle, about mid-way between the goal line and the centre of the circle. They are not defended.

As the umpire calls "play", three passing options should be available for the shooter taking the throw in. The shooter in the circle offers first, and the wing attack and centre provide alternative moves if the shooter is well defended. The shooter passes the ball to the most appropriate offer, then quickly enters the goal circle and offers strongly in the opposite direction to the other shooter.

Success Goal = 3 successful goals shot from throw ins that are taken near the post ___

Success Check

• Options are easy to read ___
• Offers are well-timed ___
• Pass is accurate ___

To Increase Difficulty

• Add the defending players to the outside feeders.
• Add another floating defender to produce an overload situation. In this case, change the success goal to two consecutive goals from baseline throw ins.

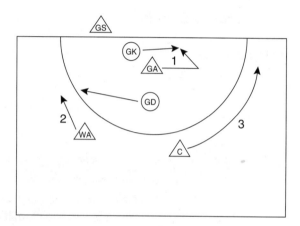

7. Sideline

To begin the drill, centre takes the sideline throw in. One defender is outside the circle and one inside, and they float rather than pressure specific players. As the centre steps up behind the line, the goal shooter reminds the attack which plan is operating. For example, the goal attack has the lead. The centre calls "play" to start the drill. The goal attack offers first. The ball is worked quickly onto the court to the goal attack and then on into the circle where the goal shooter takes a shot.

Success Goal = 3 consecutive goals scored from sideline throw ins ____

Success Check
• Use space wisely ____
• Offer strongly ____
• Pass accurately ____

To Increase Difficulty
• Add a third defender who pressures the throw in.
• Add the fourth defender and try to achieve the success goal with a full defence operating.

FRONT THIRD SUCCESS SUMMARY

Your attack end needs to combine well together to produce winning netball. Plan your attacking moves to give players a basic road map. It allows all players to understand their specific roles more easily, but does not limit their individual talents. The team that can add individual flair to a sound basic plan is difficult to beat.

RATING YOUR PROGRESS

The following self-rating chart will help you judge your overall progress to this point. Read each item carefully and respond as objectively as possible. Rate your performance by writing a number in the space provided to the right of each netball skill or tactic. After completing the inventory, assess your strengths and weaknesses, set new goals and objectives and continue to improve your play.

Rating Points: 4 = Outstanding, **3** = Good, **2** = Fair, **1** = Poor

Fundamental Skills

Your first success goal in netball is to develop the skills needed to play the game. Rate yourself on the following skills.

Catching Skills
  Two-Handed
    Above the head ____
    Chest height ____
    Below the waist ____
    Right side ____
    Left side ____
  One-Handed
    Above the head ____
    Chest height ____
    Below the waist ____
    Right side ____
    Left side ____
Toss Up
    Snatch ____
    Top-and-tail grip ____
Passing Skills
  Two-Handed Passes
    Chest pass ____
    Bounce pass ____
    Overhead pass ____
    Side pass, right ____
    Side pass, left ____
    Baulk ____

One-Handed Passes
    Shoulder pass ____
    Lob ____
    Bullet pass ____
    Underarm pass ____
    Bounce pass ____
Footwork Skills
    Take-off ____
    Running ____
    Changing direction ____
    Sidestep ____
    Jumping from one foot ____
    Jumping from two feet ____
    Landing on one foot ____
    Landing on two feet ____
    Pivot to right ____
    Pivot to left ____
    Stepping-on from two-foot landing ____
    Stepping-on from one-foot landing ____
    Recovery step ____
Shooting Skills
    Technique ____
    Accuracy ____

BISHOP BURTON COLLEGE
LIBRARY

Attacking Moves
Drive _____
Dodge ___
Fake ___
Hold ___
Roll ___
Elevate_
Combining 2 moves ___
Combining 3 moves ___
Double-play ___

Defending
One-on-one front stance ___
One-on-one back stance ___
One-on-one side stance ___
Pressuring the pass ___
Anticipating the pass ___
Defending off the player ___
Double-defence ___
Defending the down-court space ___

Tactics

To improve your level of performance in netball you must also understand, and be able to execute, the tactics used on an individual, in a group and in a team. Rate your ability to use and understand the following individual and group tactics in a game situation. Note that an assessment of team tactics is not listed since it depends on the group as a whole.

Individual Attack Tactics
Vary your moves ___
Create space for yourself ___
Select the right pass ___
Pass ahead to space ___
Time your move well ___

Group Attack Tactics
See the first move ___
Know where the backup move is ___

Individual Defence Tactics
Select appropriate starting position ___
Maintain pressure ___
Recover to legal distance ___
Anticipate and intercept pass ___

Group Defence Tactics
Three-person press ___
Centre-court press ___

Specialist Play: Skills and Tactics

To be a very good netballer you need to develop some special skills and tactics for the area of the court in which you play most frequently. Rate your ability to use the following skills and tactics in the game situation.

Back Third: Defence
Skills
Rebounding ___
Defending the shot: the lean ___
Defending the shot: the jump ___
Tactics
Splitting the circle ___
One-on-one ___
Double-defence ___

Centre Third: Starting and Linking
Attacking the Centre Pass
From the line ___
From a split ___
From a wide start ___
Using the back door ___
Defending the Centre Pass
Double-defence ___
Hold your position ___
Pressure the pass ___
Linking
Link attack play ___
Link defence play ___

Front Third: Attack
Skills
Circle awareness ____
Rebounding ____
Edging closer for a shot ____

Tactics
Shooter has the circle ____
Alternate lead ____
Deep shooters ____
Closed circle ____
Split lead ____
Double-play ____

Rules of the Game

Now rate your knowledge of the rules of the game. If you understand them well you should be able to avoid giving away a lot of penalties.

Playing positions for your team ____
Advantage ____
Centre pass ____
Contact ____
Correct distance ____
Defending a pass or shot ____
Obstruction ____

Out of court ____
Over a third ____
Penalty pass or shot ____
Replayed ball ____
Scoring a goal ____
Footwork Rule ____

Overall Netball Progress

Considering your competency in all of the skills and tactics and your knowledge of the rules listed previously, how would you rate your overall progress?

____ Outstanding
____ Good
____ Fair
____ Needs work
____ Needs a lot of work

APPENDIX: NETBALL RULES

Obtain a copy of the official rule book for a detailed explanation of the game. A summary of the main rules and modifications for beginner players is provided here.

The Game

At the senior level the game is played over 4 quarters of 15 minutes each, with a 3 minute interval between the first and second and between the third and fourth quarters, and a 5 minute interval at half time. The scorer records each goal scored, all unsuccessful shots, and the all centre passes. The scorer also calls the centre pass if asked by the umpire. Two umpires control the game. Before the match begins they toss to determine which goal end they will control.

The timekeeper takes the time from start of play, signals the end of play, and ensures that time lost through a stoppage is played in the quarter or half in which it occurred. A maximum stoppage of 5 minutes is allowed for an injury before play must resume. During a stoppage other players must remain on court and no coaching is permitted.

A team consists of seven players whose positions determine their on-court playing area. See "The Game of Netball."

The captains toss for the choice of goal end or centre pass and notify the umpires of the result. They also notify umpires and the opposing captain of changes to players' positions and any substitutions that occur. Three substitutions may be used in a game. They can be made during an interval or through injury or illness.

To start play, the centre who is taking the centre pass has the ball in the centre circle. The opposing centre is free to move in the centre third. All other players are in their respective goal thirds. The umpire's whistle starts play. The centre pass shall be caught or touched by any player who is standing or who lands within the centre third. The centre pass starts and restarts play after each goal and each interval; it alternates between both teams throughout the game.

Injuries

When play stops for an injury, the umpire restarts play from the spot where the ball was stopped. The team that was in possession of the ball takes the pass as the umpire indicates.

Advantage

The umpire does not whistle an infringement when it would be a disadvantage to the non-offending team. The umpire may use the call "advantage" to indicate this.

Contact

Contact that interferes with play is penalised, whether it is made by a player or with the ball. This means you cannot push, trip, bump or knock your opponent, particularly when defending. A Penalty Pass or a Penalty Pass or Shot is given for an infringement of the personal contact rule. Any player allowed in the area may take the penalty pass. If the contact occurs in the goal circle, the penalty is a Penalty Pass or a Penalty Pass or Shot. Either shooter can take the penalty.

Discipline

The umpire has the authority to penalise any action not covered in the rules that is contrary to the spirit of the game. Umpires may also penalise, or in exceptional circumstances, suspend players, for rough or dangerous play or misconduct.

Footwork Rule

The Footwork Rule states that you cannot re-ground your landed foot while you have possession of the ball. A detailed explanation of this rule is in Step 3.

Modification

Allow shuffling on the spot to gain balance before throwing or shooting.

Free Pass, Penalty Pass, or Penalty Pass or Shot

A free pass is awarded for most infringements other than contact or obstruction. These incur a penalty pass except when awarded in the goal circle, when a penalty shot is allowed. A penalty pass is more severe than a free pass as the offending player is literally removed from play; the infringer must stand beside the thrower taking the penalty until the ball has left the thrower's hands.

Obstruction

Any effort to defend a player with the ball from a distance closer than the correct distance (0.9 metres/3 feet) is obstruction. If you use outstretched arms to defend a player without the ball and you are closer than the correct distance, or if you use an intimidating movement against an opponent, you are also obstructing. The correct distance is measured on the ground between the nearer foot of the defender and the first landed foot of the attacker. If the attacker lessens the specified distance, then you are not considered to be obstructing; the attacker must accept the disadvantage of moving closer to the defender. Obstruction incurs the same penalty as contact: a Penalty Pass or Penalty Pass or Shot.

Offside

You are offside if you enter any area other than your designated playing area. However you may reach over and take the ball from an offside area provided you do not contact the playing area.

The penalty for offside is a free pass to the opposing team. The free pass is taken in the area in which the players went offside. A player who can enter the offside area takes the penalty where the infringement occurred. When two opposing players go offside but neither touches the ball, they are not penalised. If one or both of them are in possession of the ball or touch it, a toss-up is taken in their own area of play between those two players except when a player who is allowed only in the goal third goes offside into the center third, and an opposing player simultaneously goes offside into the goal third. A Two Up is then taken in the center third between any two opposing players allowed in that area.

Out of Court

The ball is out of court when it touches the ground, an object or a person in contact with the ground outside the court. It is also considered out of court when held by a player who is in contact with the ground outside the court.

Over a Third

The ball may not be thrown over a complete third without being touched by a player in that third. You are considered to have thrown from the third in which you gained possession, even if you step into the next third as you throw. When the ball is thrown over a third without being touched, a free pass is given to the opposing team just beyond the second line that the ball has crossed.

Playing the Ball

You have possession of the ball when you have control of it with one or two hands. If you do not catch it cleanly, you may bat or bounce it once to gain possession or to direct it to another player. Once you have possession you have three seconds in which to pass or shoot for goal. You may not punch, roll, kick, or fall on the ball, nor play the ball in any way while you are on the ground.

Once you have passed the ball you may not play it again until it is touched by another player, except after an unsuccessful shot for goal when you can try to regain possession after the ball has touched the ring. A free pass is awarded to the opposing team for any infringement of this rule.

Modification

The ball may be held for up to six seconds.

Scoring a Goal

Your team's shooters have three seconds from the time they take possession of the ball within in the goal circle to release a shot for goal. A goal is scored when the ball is thrown or batted over and completely through the goal ring by the goal shooter or goal attack. Each goal counts for one point. If a shot for goal is deflected by a defender but then passes through the goal ring, a goal is scored.

If the shot for goal is unsuccessful and the ball rebounds into court, play continues. If the ball goes out of court, then a throw in is taken where the ball crossed the line.

Modification

The shot must be released within six seconds.

The Toss Up

The toss up is used when opposing players infringe simultaneously, gain possession simultaneously, or when the umpire is uncertain who last touched the ball before it went out of court. It is taken as near as possible to the spot where the incident occurred. Players taking the toss up face each other and their own goal ends, with their arms straight and hands by their sides. The nearer foot shall be no closer than 0.9 metres (3 feet) from your opponent.

The umpire releases the ball midway between both players from just below the shoulder level of the shorter player's normal standing position. The whistle is blown as the ball is released. The ball may be caught or batted except directly at an opponent.

The Throw In

When the ball goes out of court it is thrown in by an opponent of the team that was last to touch it. To throw the ball in, stand outside the court, immediately behind the line close to the point where the ball crossed. You should pause before throwing and wait for the umpire to call "play", which indicates that all players are on court and play can restart. You must pass the ball within three seconds of this call, and the ball must leave your hands before you re-enter the court. The penalty for breaking any of these rules is a throw in to the opposing team at the spot where the infringement occurred.

Umpire's Signals

STEPPING

OBSTRUCTION

PERSONAL CONTACT

HELD BALL

OFFSIDES

TOSS UP

TAKE TIME

DIRECTION OF PASS

GOAL SCORED

ADVANTAGE

Glossary

Attack—a team or individual attacks when in possession of the ball and attempting to move it down court to their shooters.

Baulk (fake or feint)—terms to describe the action that players use when they appear to be about to release a pass but do not let go of the ball.

Centre circle—a circle that marks the centre of the court. It is 0.9 metres (3 feet) in diameter.

Centre pass—the pass that starts and restarts play after each goal is scored or after an interval.

Cushioning the impact of the landing—using your knees and ankles to reduce the jarring forces generated by landing.

Defence—a team or individual resisting attack. A team defends when it does not have possession of the ball.

Front/back half of circle—if you divide the goal circle in two by drawing a line from baseline to baseline through the midpoint of the circle, the front half is nearest the goalpost and the back half furthest away from the goalpost.

Goal circle—a semi-circle with a radius of 4.9 metres (16 feet) that radiates from the goalpost. The shooters must have possession of the ball and be wholly within the goal circle before they can shoot for goal.

Intercept—cutting off a pass from the opposing team.

Landing foot—the foot that first makes contact with the ground when a player who has possession of the ball lands. If both feet land simultaneously the player can choose the landing foot.

Long ball—a ball that travels the length or width of a third.

Obstruction—any attempt to defend a player who has possession of the ball from less than the correct distance. Obstruction is also defending a player who does not have possession of the ball with outstretched arms in less than the correct distance. Making intimidating movements to a player with or without the ball is also regarded as obstruction.

Offer—your first attacking move, also called your lead.

Preliminary move—a move used to clear space before you offer your attacking move. The fake and roll are often used in this context.

Recovery step—the step a defender takes to clear to the correct distance when the first attempt to defend has been unsuccessful.

Reground the landed foot—you replace the landed foot onto the ground while you still have possession of the ball. This is an infringement of the Footwork Rule.

Re-offer—when your lead or offer is not used and you make another move.

Shooter (Goaler)—one of the team's two players who can score goals: the goal shooter or the goal attack.

Shuffle—a small half step which is taken forwards or backwards and used in shooting drills.

Specialist session—a training session that focuses on the specific third of the court that the player works in: defence, centre or attack.

Stepping—infringing the Footwork Rule.

Stepping on—taking full advantage of the Footwork Rule to take a step and three quarters before you dispose of the ball.

Substitute—replacing a team member during the game.

Transverse line—a line that divides the court into three equal parts: a centre third and two goal thirds. There are two transverse lines on the netball court.

Throw in—restarting play when the ball has been thrown out of court. A throw in is awarded against the team that last had contact with the ball.

Toss up—a contest between two players in which the first player to catch a ball thrown into the air is the winner for the team. The ball is put into play from a toss up when two players infringe simultaneously or when the umpire is unsure just who was last to contact a ball that has gone out of court. Both players face each other and their own goal. The umpire releases the ball between them and both players quickly attempt to gain possession.

Turnover—when the defending team takes possession of the ball from the attacking team.

About the Author

Wilma Shakespear is the director of the Queensland Academy of Sport, a major high-performance center for more than 500 world-class athletes in Australia. Her contributions to the sport of netball include a world championship as a player and two as a coach, as well as pioneering work as the first head coach of netball at the Australian Institute of Sport. In this position Shakespear was the world's first professional coach of an elite netball program. At 26, she was also the youngest national coach ever appointed in Australia.

Shakespear has also made significant contributions to the advancement of women's sports in Australia and throughout the world. She originated the Women's Coaching Development Program at the Australian Institute of Sport and served on the steering committee for the "Sportswomen Step Forward" Conference in 1991. She is a founding member of Womensport Queensland, a group of sportswomen working to raise the profile and achievement of women in sport. For her continuing efforts Shakespear received the Order of Merit from the Australian Institute of Sport as well as her country's coveted Order of Australia.

Wilma Shakespear lives in Brisbane with her husband, Peter, and her children, Susan and David. Her leisure activities include gardening, painting, and renovations.

*You'll find
other outstanding
Steps to Success
resources at*

www.HumanKinetics.com

In the U.S. call

1-800-747-4457

Australia	08 8277 1555
Canada	1-800-465-7301
Europe	+44 (0) 113 255 5665
New Zealand	0064 9 448 1207

HUMAN KINETICS
The Premier Publisher for Sports & Fitness
P.O. Box 5076 • Champaign, IL 61825-5076 USA